FOREWORD BY T. MICHAE

The Future Belongs to Students in High Gear

A GUIDE FOR STUDENTS AND ASPIRING GAME CHANGERS
IN TRANSITION FROM COLLEGE TO CAREER

AMY D. HOWELL & ANNE DEETER GALLAHER

Printed in the United States of America
First Printing, 2015
ISBN 13: 978-0-692-38088-8
ISBN 10: 0-692-38088-4

www.StudentsInHighGear.com
Twitter.com/StudentsInHG

Cover design by Rick Snizik.
Book design by Gennifer Richie.

To curious students and game changers everywhere who want their education and life to make a difference. We hope our insights add direction to your college experience and help you connect the dots along the way to achieve success—in life, in your career, and in your community. High gear awaits!

AMY & ANNE

Acclaim

FOR *STUDENTS IN HIGH GEAR*

"*Higher education has never been under more scrutiny and pressure to clearly articulate the value-add of a college degree and its relationship to a career trajectory.* Students in High Gear *fills a gap for students exploring how to make the most of college, how to get the best return on their substantial investment, and how to lay a solid foundation for success.*"

DR. MICHAEL DAVID RUDD
President, The University of Memphis

"*A friend of mine said, 'Mediocrity is mass produced. Destiny is custom designed.' Success is no different; it all depends on how the students define success. Books such as* Students in High Gear *provide a first-hand account of what it takes to conquer the college landscape, and this book will act as a experiential multiplier to assist students in realizing their goals for success. When students give their testimonials and insights as to what nurtured their path to triumph, there could not be a better playbook.*"

DR. BOB AKIN
Assistant Professor of Professional Practice, Texas Christian University

"Students in High Gear *is a perfectly timed book. At a time when society is questioning the value of colleges and universities, this book helps to clarify the importance of education along with core values that all engaged students and future leaders should have in their tool kit.*"

DR. RUSSELL WIGGINTON
Vice President for the Office of External Programs, Rhodes College

"*Amy Howell and Anne Deeter Gallaher are accomplished communications professionals who could have written a valuable book from their combined expertise and experiences.*

In Students in High Gear, *they've done that—and more. Amy and Anne have included the voices and experiences of students themselves. These young people—some in college, some just graduated—add immediacy to the book's wise observations and savvy advice.*

There are paths, and tools, to college and early career success. Some are time-tested (connect broadly with teachers and fellow students); others are newly relevant (curate your digital footprint with care). In Students in High Gear, *Amy and Anne share a broad range of practical guidance for students, their parents—and yes, teachers too.*

In the rapidly evolving media world in which I work, we would welcome Students in High Gear!"

KATHLEEN A. PAVELKO
President & CEO, WITF Public Media

"*We add our voice to Amy and Anne's as we reach out to high school and college students: Seize the opportunity, the future is yours. Demographic trends, primarily the retirement of the Baby Boomers, are leaving a big hole to fill in today's workforce. That doesn't mean that you don't have to work to find a good job, but for the right young people with the right mix of knowledge, communication skills, and self-confidence in your own abilities,* Students in High Gear *will start you in the right direction. Businesses and entire regions are marketing to young people to attract their business or to consider living and working in their region. Competitive regions of the future will have the workforce of the future, it only makes sense.*

Competition is part of life and making yourself more competitive and more marketable is what this book is about. Employers are looking for young employees in high gear, young people who can immediately make contributions to a business, and add ideas and value to a community. Students in High Gear *is about the future and how to shift into high gear to be a successful part of that future.*"

DAVID E. BLACK
President & CEO, Harrisburg Regional Chamber & CREDC

Table of Contents

Foreword

BY T. MICHAEL GLENN
EXECUTIVE VICE PRESIDENT
CHIEF MARKETING AND SALES OFFICER
FEDEX CORPORATION

I vividly remember entering my final semester of college. I prepared my resume and signed up for on-campus interviews with the expectation of multiple job offers to choose from. The problem was I was only asked to interview by a couple of companies. My resume simply did not measure up. My summer work experience could hardly be considered internships as we know them today, and my resume lacked the type of community involvement activities that companies found attractive. I had one job offer selling tires in a retail store 500 miles from home. I left college unemployed and was definitely not in high gear.

While I was able to overcome the slow start to my career, the challenges facing young people today are even more daunting. I cringe every time I see an ill-advised photo or post on Twitter or Facebook, with no consideration that it will forever become part of a digital resume. Development of a personal brand, like it or not, starts with your first engagement on social media. Have a plan, and be thoughtful in how you use social media. To borrow an old saying, If you don't want to read about it in the paper tomorrow morning, don't post it.

"Dot-Connecting and Why You Must Master It" is one of my favorite chapters in *Students in High Gear*. Building a network early and including friends, professors, and professional acquaintances is critical. Given how competitive the job market is today, in many cases it is not what you know, it is who you know that will make the difference. Volunteering for a local charity is a great example of connecting the dots. Typically, charitable organizations have leaders and board members that are well-connected in their communities and may be able to open a door for you in the future.

I am often asked what I look for when evaluating young professionals. The answer is simple: I look for an individual that is viewed as a leader among peers. My definition of leadership is the ability to motivate a diverse group of people to accomplish a common goal. Study groups, church groups, and social organizations all provide opportunities to hone leadership skills.

I also look for how an individual carries himself or herself day to day. Take dress for example. When I joined FedEx over 30 years ago, I was given a copy of the book *Dress for Success*. The formula was pretty straightforward—blue or gray suit, starched shirt, and matching tie. Today, casual dress complicates things and this does matter in business. One person's definition of casual is another person's definition of sloppy. My advice is to dress for high gear. Don't wear worn out, torn, or ill-fitting clothes. Seek professionalism in your dress code as well as everything else, and consider being overdressed instead of underdressed or poorly dressed.

As you read this book, I hope you will take note of the fundamentals that are so clearly outlined. When applied, these fundamentals will definitely launch you into high gear!

Preface

THE LANDSCAPE OF HIGHER EDUCATION
IN THE UNITED STATES 2015

Who are today's college students? And how large of a group are we talking about?

To create a framework for a conversation about *Students in High Gear*, we dove into some research on higher education in the United States. Our findings will help you form a fuller picture of who goes to college, the gender breakdown for college graduates, the schools that are hot spots for specific careers, current costs of attending college, degrees granted, private versus public institutions, and graduation rates.

For example, the projected enrollment for students—this includes undergraduate, graduate, and professional students—in the fall of 2014 was 21 million (National Center for Education Statistics). According to The World Bank, there are 158.9 million people ages 15 and older in the U.S. labor force who are classified as economically active. So the cohort we are writing to comprises nearly 20% of that population.

If a college education is a great equalizer—and we feel that it is—then the 21 million higher ed student population is a group we need to encourage and engage in high gear opportunities to grow and create jobs. Economically active and in high gear are where "changing your stars" takes place.

THE STATS:
Top schools that graduate entrepreneurs, engineers, IT, business, law, medicine, education:

Top 5 schools for entrepreneurs: Babson College (Wellesley, MA), University of Houston (Houston, TX), Baylor University (Waco, TX), Brigham Young University (Provo, UT), University of Oklahoma (Norman, OK) [Forbes 2014].

Top 5 schools for engineers: Massachusetts Institute of Technology (Cambridge, MA), Stanford University (Stanford, CA), University of California-Berkeley (Berkeley, CA), California Institute of Technology (Pasadena, CA), and Carnegie Mellon University (Pittsburgh, PA) [U.S. News Education].

Top 5 schools for information and technology management: Carnegie Mellon University (Pittsburgh, PA), Syracuse University (Syracuse, NY), University at Albany-SUNY (Albany, NY), Rutgers (Newark, NJ), and Georgia Institute of Technology (Atlanta, GA) [U.S. News Education].

Top 5 schools for business: Tied for first are Harvard University (Cambridge, MA), Stanford University (Stanford, CA), and Wharton University (Philadelphia, PA), fourth is Booth School of Business (Chicago, IL), and fifth is Sloan School of Management at Massachusetts Institute of Technology (Cambridge, MA) [U.S. News Education].

Top 5 schools for law: Yale University (New Haven, CT), Harvard University (Cambridge, MA), Stanford University (Stanford, CA), Columbia University (New York, NY), and University of Chicago (Chicago, IL) [U.S. News Education].

Top 5 schools for medicine research: Harvard University (Boston, MA), Stanford University (Stanford, CA), Johns Hopkins University (Baltimore, MD), University of California-San Francisco (San Francisco, CA), and University of Pennsylvania (Philadelphia, PA) [U.S. News Education].

Top 5 schools for education: Johns Hopkins University (Baltimore, MD), Vanderbilt University (Nashville, TN), Harvard University (Cambridge, MA), Stanford University (Stanford, CA), and University of Pennsylvania (Philadelphia, PA) [U.S. News Education].

How many college students are in the U.S.?

As of 2013, 14,473,884 undergraduate students enrolled in colleges and universities. The graduate student population consisted of 2,097,511 people (National Center for Education Statistics, 2013). The projected enrollment for students (undergraduate, graduate, and professional) in the fall of 2014 was 21 million (National Center for Education Statistics, 2014).

How many public versus private colleges and universities?

As of 2013, the number of public 4-year institutions totaled 629, public 2-year institutions totaled 1,070, private 4-year institutions totaled 1,845, and private 2-year institutions totaled 596, which amounts to 4,140 U.S. colleges and universities (National Center for Education Statistics, 2014).

How many students are in 2-year institutions?

In 2013, 6,184,229 students enrolled in a public 2-year institution and 303,826 students enrolled in a private 2-year institution (National Center for Education Statistics, 2013). The National Center for Education Statistics predicted 7.3 million students would enroll in 2-year institutions for the 2014–2015 school year.

How many students are in 4-year institutions?

In 2013, public 4-year institution and private 4-year institution enrollment rates were 6,837,605 students and 4,161,815 students, respectively (National Center for Education Statistics, 2013). An estimated 13.7 million students were intended to enroll in 4-year institutions in the 2014–2015 school term (National Center for Education Statistics, 2014). By comparison, in 2015, there are 110,000 students enrolled in the Pennsylvania State System of Higher Education.

What is the average cost of a college education?

"For the 2012–2013 academic year, the average annual price for undergraduate tuition, fees, room, and board was $15,022 at public institutions, $39,173 at private nonprofit institutions, and $23,158 at private for-profit institutions. Charges for tuition and required fees averaged $5,899 at public institutions, $28,569 at private nonprofit institutions, and $13,766 at private for-profit institutions," (National Center for Education Statistics, 2014).

According to The College Board, the average price for tuition, fees, room, and board for the 2013–2014 academic year was $10,781 at public 2-year in-district institutions, $18,383 at public 4-year in-state institutions, $31,721 at public 4-year out-of-state institutions, and $40,955 at private nonprofit 4-year institutions. For the 2014–2015 academic year, the average price was $11,052 at public 2-year in-district institutions (2.5% change), $18,943 at public 4-year in-state institutions (3.0% change), $32,762 at public 4-year out-of-state institutions (3.3% change), and $42,419 at private nonprofit 4-year institutions (3.6% change).

"The average published tuition and fee price for full-time out-of-state students at public 4-year institutions is about 2.5 times as high as the price for in-state students," (The College Board, 2015).

About two-thirds of undergraduate students enrolled full-time in 2011–2012 received grants that reduced the actual price of college (NCES, NPSAS, 2012). In addition, many states and institutions grant tuition waivers to groups such as veterans, teachers, or dependents of employees (The College Board, 2015).

Enrollment breakdown for men and women attending college

Women outpace men in college attendance and statisticians anticipate the gap to increase in the coming years. In the 2013–2014 academic year, the percentage of women enrolled at universities and colleges was 57.4% (National Center for Education Statistics, 2014). *Forbes*, utilizing information from the U.S. Bureau of Statistics, noted a 45–55 men-to-women ratio existed in 2005; however, in 2008 it appeared the ratio was pushing toward a 40–60 men-to-women ratio (Borzelleca, 2012).

"According to the Census Bureau, 685,000 men and 916,000 women graduated from college in 2009. . . . That means 25% fewer men received college degrees than women," (Jeffrey, 2012).

Number of students who take 5 years to graduate?

According to Scott-Clayton (2011), "even among graduates who continuously attend full time, 45% need an extra year or more to finish." Scott-Clayton stated overcrowding might be a potential reason for the extension in time at university in that students cannot take the courses they need. Another supposed reason is that "colleges [do not] have much incentive to get students out any faster" in that they are encouraged to explore electives.

Kertscher (2013) analyzed the U.S. Department of Education statistics that "cover students who earned their first four-year degree during the 2007–2008 school year. . . . They include part-time as well as full-time students; students who started their college studies at a 2-year or a 4-year institution; and students who were not seeking a degree of any type when they initially entered college. For that relatively broad collection of students, the average time to get their bachelor's degree was 6 years and 4 months." Kertscher further assessed "the time was shorter—5 years and 10 months—for students who began college within a year of finishing high school." Basic percentages reported by Kertscher included 23% of students needed 5 or 6 years and 33% who took more than 6 years.

According to U.S. News Education (2015), the top 5 schools where students graduated in 4 years who started in 2007 include Franklin W. Olin College of Engineering (Needham, MA) with a 93% graduation rate, Pomona College (Claremont, CA) with a

93% graduation rate, Fashion Institute of Design & Merchandising (Los Angeles, CA) with a 91% graduation rate, Haverford College (Haverford, PA) with a 91% graduation rate, and Amherst College (Amherst, MA) with a 90% graduation rate.

Degrees awarded annually

National Center for Education Statistics (2013) have the following statistics relating to degrees awarded annually: associate degrees 696,660, bachelor's degrees 1,439,264, master's degrees 574,618, doctorate degrees 52,631, and professional degrees 87,289.

"During the 2014–2015 school year, colleges and universities are expected to award 1 million associate's degrees; 1.8 million bachelor's degrees; 821,000 master's degrees; and 177,500 doctor's degrees," (National Center for Education Statistics, 2014).

State with the highest and lowest number of college graduates

According to the U.S. Census Bureau of Statistics of 2003, the region with the highest attainment of bachelor's degrees was the Northeast with 30.3%, followed by the Western region with 28.7%, the Midwest region with 26%, and the Southern region with 25.3%.

Frohlich, Serenbetz, Kent, and Hess (2014) reported, "More than 40% of Massachusetts residents had at least a bachelor's degree, the highest percentage nationwide." In addition, West Virginia had the lowest level of college graduates with 18.9% of adults 25 and older having attained at least a bachelor's degree (Frohlich, Serenbetz, Kent, and Hess, 2014).

How hard is it for college graduates to find a job?

Weissmann (2014) stated, "The Economic Policy Institute reported that roughly 8.5% of college graduates between the ages of 21 and 24 were unemployed." Further, "the EPI finds that a total of 16.8% of new grads are 'unemployed,' meaning they're either jobless and hunting for work; working part-time because they can't find a full-time job; or want a job, have looked within the past year, but have now given up on searching."

Analysts for the New York Federal Reserve Bank "found that roughly 6% of recent college graduates, aged 22 to 27, were unemployed at the beginning of 2013 and 44% were underemployed," (Hechinger Report, 2014).

The Bureau of Labor Statistics (2014) created a chart which lists the unemployment rate in 2013 as follows: doctoral degree is 2.2%, professional degree is 2.3%, master's degree is 3.4%, bachelor's degree is 4.0%, associate's degree is 5.4%, some college/no degree is 7.0%, high school diploma is 7.5%, and less than a high school diploma is 11%.

How many college graduates are living at home?

Gallup Daily (2014) reported, "14% of adults between the ages of 24 and 34—those in the post-college years when most young adults are trying to establish independence—report living at home with their parents." Furthermore, 29% of all U.S. adults under age 35 report living at home.

Weissmann (2013) asked and answered the question: "What share of recent college graduates were living with family in 2011? It's 45%." Weissmann included a graph by the Pew Research Center that indicated in 2011, 21% of college graduates aged 18 to 34 lived at home.

Number of college graduates who have jobs and the earnings differential

"In 2012, about 73% of young adults ages 25–34 with a bachelor's or higher degree in the labor force had year-round, full-time jobs, compared with 65% of those with an associate's degree, 59% of those with some college education, 60% of high school completers, and 49% of those without a high school diploma or its equivalent," (National Center for Education Statistics, 2014).

"In 2012, the median earnings for full-time, year-round working young adults aged 25–34 with a bachelor's degree was $46,900, while the median was $22,900 for those without a high school diploma or its equivalent, $30,000 for those with a high school diploma or its equivalent, and $35,700 for those with an associate's degree. **In other words, young adults with a bachelor's degree earned more than twice as much as those without a high school diploma or its equivalent (105% more) and 57% more than young adult high school completers.** Additionally, in 2012 the median earnings for young adults with a master's degree or higher was $59,600, some 27% more than the median for young adults with a bachelor's degree," (National Center for Education Statistics, 2014).

REFERENCES

Adams, Susan. (2014). "The Top 50 Schools for Entrepreneurs." Forbes. <http://www.forbes.com/sites/susanadams/2014/09/19/the-top-50-schools-for-entrepreneurs/>.

Borzelleca, Daniel. (2012). "The Male-Female Ratio in College." Forbes. <http://www.forbes.com/sites/ccap/2012/02/16/the-male-female-ratio-in-college/>.

Bureau of Labor Statistics. (2014). "Employment Projections." United States Department of Labor. <http://www.bls.gov/emp/ep_chart_001.htm>.

Frolich, Thomas C., Serenbetz, Robert, Kent, Alexander, & Hess, Alexander E.M. (2014). "America's Most (and Least) Educated States." <http://247wallst.com/special-report/2014/09/23/americas-most-and-least-educated-states/>.

Hechinger Report. (2014). "Reflections on the underemployment of college graduates." Education by the Numbers. <http://educationbythenumbers.org/content/underemployment-college-grads_1589/>.

Jeffrey, Terence P. (2012). "25% Fewer Men Than Women Graduate College; Obama: It's 'A Great Accomplishment . . . For America.'" CNSNews. <http://cnsnews.com/news/article/25-fewer-men-women-graduate-college-obama-its-great-accomplishment-america>.

Jones, Jeffrey M. (2014). "In U.S., 14% of Those Aged 24 to 34 Are Living With Parents." Gallup. <http://www.gallup.com/poll/167426/aged-living-parents.aspx>.

Kertscher, Tom. (2013). "On average, a college degree takes six years, U.S. Sen. Ron Johnson says." PolitiFact. <http://www.politifact.com/wisconsin/statements/2013/aug/11/ron-johnson/average-college-degree-takes-six-years-us-sen-ron-/>.

National Center for Education Statistics. (2013). "College Enrollment Statistics." <http://www.statisticbrain.com/college-enrollment-statistics/>.

National Center for Education Statistics. (2014). "Fast Facts."
<http://nces.ed.gov/fastfacts/display.asp?id=372>.

Scott-Clayton, Judith. (2011). "The Rise of the Five-Year Four-Year Degree." The New York Times. <http://economix.blogs.nytimes.com/2011/05/20/the-rise-of-the-five-year-four-year-degree/?_r=0>.

The College Board. (2015). "Trends in Higher Education."
<http://trends.collegeboard.org/college-pricing/figures-tables/average-published-undergraduate-charges-sector-2014-15>.

U.S. Census Bureau. (2003). "Educational Attainment in the United States: 2003."
<http://trends.collegeboard.org/college-pricing/figures-tables/average-published-undergraduate-charges-sector-2014-15>.

U.S. News Education. (2014). "U.S. News Releases 2015 Best Graduate Schools Rankings." <http://www.usnews.com/education/best-graduate-schools/articles/2014/03/11/us-news-releases-2015-best-graduate-schools-rankings>.

U.S. News Education. (2015). "Best Engineering Schools."
<http://grad-schools.usnews.rankingsandreviews.com/best-graduate-schools/top-engineering-schools/eng-rankings>.

U.S. News Education. (2015). "Best Information and Technology Management."
<http://grad-schools.usnews.rankingsandreviews.com/best-graduate-schools/top-public-affairs-schools/information-technology-management-rankings>.

U.S. News Education. (2015). "Highest 4-Year Graduation Rates."
<http://colleges.usnews.rankingsandreviews.com/best-colleges/rankings/highest-grad-rate>.

Weissmann, Jordan. (2013). "Here's Exactly How Many College Graduates Live Back at Home." The Atlantic. <http://www.theatlantic.com/business/archive/2013/02/heres-exactly-how-many-college-graduates-live-back-at-home/273529/>.

Weissmann, Jordan. (2014). "How Bad Is the Job Market for the College Class of 2014?" Slate. <http://www.slate.com/blogs/moneybox/2014/05/08/unemployment_and_the_class_of_2014_how_bad_is_the_job_market_for_new_college.html>.

Introduction

If you're a college student today, we are excited to welcome you to the business world and help you put your education to work. If you're a high school student, we earnestly hope the experiences in our book will challenge you to study harder, set high gear goals, and make good decisions. The world is your stage!

A student's performance starts young and is now visible to the world. By visible, we mean the world has a window to your digital footprint—the collection of content that you create on the Internet and on mobile devices. What a digital footprint says about our young people starts very early, sometimes at 11 or 12 when they have their first smartphone. Actually, children today have a digital footprint that begins with their sonogram posted on Facebook by Mom and Dad. This digital reality is just setting in and can have unintended consequences. What types of students are we training? Who is teaching them how to leverage their connections, connect the dots, and act on smart and savvy strategies that prepare them for graduating and landing in a high gear environment?

As mothers of five students collectively, business owners of public relations firms, and college graduates ourselves, we wanted to share our stories, connections, reflections, knowledge, and challenges to help students everywhere shorten your learning curves to a high gear outcome—whatever your goal may be.

We are inspired daily by the stories we hear of young students already leveraging the power of digital media for their immediate advantage. We are also concerned for the hundreds of thousands of students who are not. **Our economy and our ability to compete in a global marketplace depend greatly on the success of our students.**

Are students as prepared as they need to be? Can they do more? Do they understand the importance of good communication skills in this texting world? Do they know the importance of real-world experience and securing internships? Do they understand how to manage debt, and the importance of living like a student when they actually are students? Do they understand how to connect dots and leverage relationships? Can they graduate from college with both good grades AND work experience? Yes!

One of the best commencement speeches explaining the raw power of an education was delivered by former U.S. Secretary of State Condoleezza Rice in 2012 at Southern Methodist University in Texas.

> You see, education is transformative. It literally changes lives. That is why people work so hard to become educated. And that is why education has always been the key to human beings and their dreams—a force that erases arbitrary divisions of race and class and culture, and unlocks every person's potential.

Helping you discover and unlock your potential is one of our high gear goals.

Graduation alone is not an isolated high gear goal. Earning that degree is certainly an accomplishment; however, it is no longer a guarantee that you will secure a job. Today's students must be equipped with more knowledge, adapt to a more complex world, and find more mentors to be competitive. Recessions and depressions, slowdowns and rallies are a part of every American business. Each phase gives us an opportunity to study the DNA of thriving organizations and the type of young leaders they seek.

What types of leaders are we creating? Are they digitally savvy? How is social media being used to tell great stories to the world? Our passion is to help students achieve more through finding their high gear. Our experiences aren't generally found in textbooks or college courses, but from the offices, C-suites, and internships across American businesses. These are experiences we want to share with every stakeholder in the educational journey and with anyone who has a passion for young leader development and career advancement.

Forbes Magazine released information on graduates that earn the most money. It turns out that Ivy League schools are not at the top of the list, although they are close. Instead, the No. 1 and 2 schools are a science and technology school and a military school. According to the *Forbes Magazine* article written by Susan Adams, Harvey Mudd, a 60-year-old science and technology school with only 784 students in Claremont, CA, ranked No. 1 with grads earning a median mid-career salary of $137,800. The U.S. Naval Academy at Annapolis has a student body of 4,536 and ranked No. 2 at Academy alums earning $134,000 median salary. However, the Naval Academy comes with a five-year commitment to serve in the military, including five years of active duty. In third place was Stanford, who the article describes as "arguably the most prestigious school on the West Coast," whose mid-career grads earn approximately $133,700 annually.

We asked a number of colleges and universities to share what defines their graduates as high gear. Their stories and visions enrich our book. Also on these pages are stories of students blazing a trail to high gear. *Students in High Gear* is not packed with theory, but with practical, from-the-trenches student and business experiences.

We are certain there are many other great stories, so we hope you will chime in, tweet us, email us, comment on **www.StudentsInHighGear.com**, and let us hear from you.

Is college attainable for everyone? While we are writing this book aimed at college students and graduates, we recognize that college graduation is not a prerequisite to success. Not all leaders or executives have college degrees. However, we believe that college is a game changer and very important for your future earning potential. We believe not having a college degree can be a significant door closer for job seekers. To that end, we are also seeing older workers stay in the workforce longer and that increases the job competition. With a college degree, you have one more tool in your toolbox.

Additionally, not all graduates will become high-income earners. Steve Jobs, founder of Apple, dropped out of college and started attending classes he wanted to attend. His path was very high gear, but not one that embraced the traditional college experience. If college isn't an investment you desire, find your high gear in a trade or skill that you can apply successfully in the workforce. You can't get a haircut online, so there are many occupations that will always be in demand—welders, tile setters, plumbers, mechanics, and construction jobs—and have great potential for you to succeed and be a high gear earner.

Not everyone fits into the college track, and while we are writing here to those who see themselves in college, the world needs all types of workers and there are great opportunities for training and skill development in the technical schools. For young women and entrepreneurs, you'll find more career advice in our first book, *Women in High Gear: A Guide for Entrepreneurs, On-Rampers, and Aspiring Executives* available on Amazon.

This book springs from the countless parents who regularly ask both of us to mentor and counsel their college graduates who are job seeking. This is the best advice we have to offer, and our hope is that it helps make a difference in your high gear life and career journey. As Jonathan Winters said, "If your ship doesn't come in, swim to it." Join us in the deep end!

CHAPTER 1
What Is High Gear?

"*If you say you can or you can't*
you are right either way."

HENRY FORD

In our first book, *Women in High Gear*, we define high gear. For students, we think the same definitions apply and that success comes from making great choices, doing what is right, and not being afraid to go against the status quo.

It means reaching for a very high standard in everything you do. It means saying No to mediocrity. It means thinking big and reaching out for support to reach your goals. It means getting up early to meet an internship connection when you'd rather stay in bed. High gear is taking the path less traveled and stretching beyond your comfort zone to reach your goals. High gear is not easy. It demands focus, setting goals, making smart decisions, and developing a growth mindset.

High gear is a life journey. Think about your education as a marathon, not a sprint. Read ambitiously, engage in your classes, be curious, and dependable. This drive is a precursor to professional development opportunities at work.

High gear is defined by your character, ambition, and ability to connect the dots to leverage your success. This is not a solo journey. You will want to find mentors and seek advice. Read the success stories of others and apply their lessons to your own career journey. No two high gear stories look exactly alike. Whether your job is cleaning restrooms or closing the markets at NASDAQ, your contagious attitude, drive, and enthusiasm will attract positive attention.

AMY

High gear for me as a student meant being on my game in school—academically as well as embracing leadership opportunities. I grew up in Texas but moved to Alabama and had to adapt to a new city in the fifth grade. In middle school, I was called a geek by some of my classmates, but I never let that deter me from my goals. Because I was not naturally the most popular, that meant I had to work harder for what I wanted. I also had jobs in high school—babysitting, lifeguarding, and working in the tennis pro shop of a country club. My dad helped me open my own checking account, and I learned the importance of earning money. I didn't have a car, but I made enough money to buy necessities and start saving.

I ran for Key Club president my junior year as the first female to ever run and win—a great accomplishment for our high school and a way for me to blaze a trail for other female student leaders. I felt comfortable in a civic leadership position and worked hard organizing car washes and other fundraisers. The more leadership success I had, the more I was inspired to continue. Some of the faculty at the school encouraged me and praised our club for the good work we were doing. I think those words of encouragement from faculty are very important for students. My senior year I was selected by the Daughters of the American Revolution chapter as their scholarship recipient of the year.

High gear in high school leads to high gear in college. It also means being strategic about where you apply and thinking in terms of what you want to do *after college*. Sometimes we are too focused on getting into college, and we miss thinking longer term about our decisions. Think carefully about the size and type of college to make sure it's *your* best fit.

It is important to have goals early. High gear means making good choices when you are young that will pay dividends later. High gear also means not giving up. Don't quit a job because it is difficult. Embrace the difficult; work on mastering the difficult. Learn as much as you can. On the other hand, if a major is too difficult and you need to switch gears to another major in which you excel, that is strategic high gear problem solving. For me, switching from chemistry to English was vital if I was going to graduate!

For students at any age, high gear also means: Think for yourself, listen to your parents, do the right thing, do your best, hang out with positive people, stay away from negative people, don't let bullies win and fight them every chance you can, stand up and stand out, study hard, party less, love your family, go to church, give back and read everything you can about innovation and excellence in this world.

That is what you must do. Stay away from drugs—they are a dead end. Stay away from those who sell and do drugs. Surround yourself with other high gear people. Look for high gear. Embrace it and envision it in your future. Everything you accomplish in school has a connection to your future. Your high gear needs to be in the right gear. Listen to your teachers. Find a mentor. Connect the dots. It all matters and is relevant to success later.

Young people are in danger of losing their ability to communicate effectively due to texting, technology, and this instant-everything world we live in. It is not ok for too many OMGs and LOLs and IDKs to float around on multiple devices at my house. Students need to know how to communicate clearly; kudos to parents and teachers who are working on this now.

Another thing we have noticed is that as a society, we are seeing students at each of two extremes—overscheduled or not engaged at all—and not enough balance in the middle. High gear parenting means getting our teens involved in making better choices to fill idle time. If the answer to boredom is drinking, violence, or drugs, we are in trouble as a society as this behavior is a dead-end and a serious threat to our economy. That is why not-for-profit charities, churches, and community organizations are vital in channeling positive options for our children.

Beginning in high school, I think it's important to do things for others and get in the habit of contributing to the community outside of a classroom. Raise money for a good cause. Go paint a Habitat for Humanity house with your friends. Join a youth group at church and help feed the hungry at the local soup kitchen. Demonstrate leadership and practice it by doing these things to give back in your community.

Finally, make sure what you do counts or makes a difference. I think teens are joining groups to have fluff on an application. Recruiters want to see how you made a difference, and how it is unique. And you must also have the ability to communicate this face-to-face in an interview.

Here are some high gear tips I share with students and my own children as they navigate through high school and college:

1. Your choices are yours. Make good ones, stay busy, and listen to your inner voice.

2. Find a mentor. If your parents are not your mentors, find someone who is. If you are parenting a teen, you know that if they will not take your advice, they will listen to others.

3. Enjoy your classes and try your best. You may find your passion in one of those books or from one of your teachers. Listen to the teachers who challenge you the most.

4. Send a handwritten thank-you note to anyone who takes the time to talk with you.

5. Get a job in high school and in college. I don't care if it is cleaning tables, working in a retail store, hostessing— whatever. It helps you develop better communication skills and helps instill a work ethic early. You can also add these jobs to your resume and college application; you will stand out if you have had jobs in high school.

6. Sleep more. A recent national study by the National Academy of Pediatricians cited lack of sleep during teen years as a major threat to the U.S. and future young adults.

7. Be a leader! Join a few of the many extra-curricular activities offered by the school. Think beyond sports. The possibilities are endless.

8. Learn to play a musical instrument. This is something I didn't do and have always regretted. It's a great way to become more well-rounded and can offer many advantages.

9. Try to secure at least one business internship while you are in high school. I'm impressed by the schools that encourage high school seniors to secure some experience. I have had some great high school interns from Hutchison School in Memphis. Whether it is shadowing an executive or doing a project for a company, this early advantage can help you leapfrog your path to high gear.

10. If you know you are entrepreneurial, find a start-up and seek to get to know the people behind it. Ask to blog about it or do a school paper on the company. Interview the owner. Get an internship with a company like this and see how it fuels your passion to be an entrepreneur.

11. Read the newspapers and stay current on world events. I think it is more important than ever for high school students to understand what is happening across our world. Knowledge is leverage to a high gear journey.

ANNE

Students are the lifeblood of our U.S. economy, and I am always energized when I talk to high school and college classes. One of our chief goals for writing *Students in High Gear* is to shorten your learning curve to educational and career success. We need your energy, passion, curiosity, spirit, and big ideas to transform our marketplace.

In these chapters, we'll help you navigate this wonderful and challenging journey from student to professional. We'll help you set aspirational goals and teach you how to wisely connect the dots and develop a support system that bridges the student-to-employee status.

Some of my best professors in college were adjunct professors who had deep connections to the business community. My first internship in my junior year of college was at an ad agency, and it was the direct result of my adjunct Communications professor who brokered the opportunity for me. High gear students make sure professors know who they are.

Regardless of how big your classes are—300 in a lecture hall or 30 in a night class—introduce yourself to your professors. Ask them if you can buy them a cup of coffee and ask them some questions about the college and career transition. Take advantage of their vast experience and the thousands of connections they have. They can't help you if they don't know who you are. Anonymity is not a business or career advantage. Your professors are the best first steps to reaching high gear, securing internships, and enlarging your network.

I was invited recently to speak to a public relations class at Messiah College, in Pennsylvania, and the students asked me to name one thing that I wish I would have done differently as a college student. I didn't have to think too long about that one. I quickly answered, "I wish I would have thought about setting high gear goals much, much earlier in my educational journey. And that goes for my business career, too."

There's something powerful about putting yourself in a high gear mindset—a growth mindset. You can't make the football team if you don't try out. You can't reach Eagle Scout if you don't join the Troop. And you'll never have an internship if you don't make the ask. As Gandhi said, "What you think you become."

The common thread to all high gear students is an action that begins with the individual. You are the catalyst. You have to see yourself in high gear. High gear success is intentional. It doesn't just happen to people in school or in business. It begins with thinking about your high gear goals and seeing yourself achieve them.

Don't get in the way of your own success. A good first step is to write down high gear goals on paper and keep them in plain sight. Ask your friends to hold you accountable for working toward them. Saying your goals out loud and tweeting them lends a certain validity and power to your ideas. If you say it out loud and write it down, you've just accomplished the first step to reaching your high gear.

In our first book, *Women in High Gear*, we tell the story of Denise Morrison, CEO of Campbell Soup Company. *The Wall Street Journal* was writing an article about her family and their leadership achievements. She was quoted as saying she was going to be a CEO—not that she hoped to be a CEO. When the article ran in *The Wall Street Journal*, friends called to say, "I can't believe you said that! What if you don't become a CEO?" Ms. Morrison replied, "The thought never crossed my mind."

Don't be afraid to think big at a young age.

What do we mean by being high gear in high school? I have a good story as an example. Last year I answered a call at my office. The woman was a business teacher at a high school 30 minutes away. She introduced herself and told me how grateful she was that I took her call (she expected an admin would answer my phone).

"I am calling on behalf of one of my students, Jillian S. She just showed me a newspaper article about you and your PR firm. The article also mentioned your new book, *Women in High Gear*. Our students are expected to find an internship during their senior year, and Jillian asked if I would call you to see if you ever accept high school interns; and if you do, would you be willing to meet with her at your office to discuss the possibility."

As a business owner, I love high gear dot-connecting. I love to see young people think big and reach out to business leaders for advice and support. I was so impressed by Jillian's ability to connect the dots from my newspaper article, to her teacher, and then to making the ask that I told the teacher I would certainly consider having Jillian as an intern.

The teacher went on to say that Jillian was a wonderful young lady, president of her class for the past three years, on the Varsity field hockey team, leader of several school committees, and a straight A student. I told the teacher that based on Jillian's ability to think big and to research a company to seek an internship with, I would be happy to meet with her.

Several weeks later, an energetic, friendly, high gear young lady came to Deeter Gallaher Group with a resume and an armful of accomplishments. "I read your book and am so inspired," she said. Wow. Thinking big was her first high gear accomplishment; making the ask was her second; reading *Women in High Gear* in advance of our meeting so she could be prepared to weave it into our conversation was a home run. I accepted her as one of my interns, and she was a hard worker and a delight in the office.

Jillian gave the commencement speech at her high school graduation and invited me to join her family in the stadium. I smiled when she referenced her internship experience and how inspired she was to be a "Woman in High Gear."

When she left for Penn State University, I gave her a journal to write down her high gear goals. The first week of school she sent me a tweet that showed her goals written on page 1 of her journal: "Be the head of the PR committee for THON." I wasn't surprised by the magnitude of this goal for an 18 year old. THON is Penn State's dance marathon and the largest student-run philanthropy in the world. To lead the PR committee for such an event will require a massive investment of time, energy, collaboration, media skill, leadership, and very big ideas. I have no doubt that Jillian will lead this committee before her graduation.

Let's get started:

1. Write down three high gear goals.
2. Don't wait for permission from friends, teachers, or parents to start your high gear journey.
3. Read stories of successful people—young, old, executives, entrepreneurs, men, and women.
4. Hang with high gear friends—people who will challenge you to do better, work harder, and never give up.
5. Don't be afraid of risk, failure, or embarrassment. The road to high gear is filled with doubters, haters, ridiculers, gossip mongers, and mean-spirited people. That's the reality, so don't let the arrows stick. Keep focused on high gear.

We have asked several college students to share their high gear stories. What does it mean to them? Below we are including some content from current college students who are about to graduate and move on to the next chapter in their high gear journey. We think Kaely Johnson, a senior at Texas Christian University wrote a perfect summary of her definition of high gear.

Kaely Johnson, Senior, Texas Christian University (TCU)

The phrase high gear has a specific and personal meaning for everyone that hears the term. Coming from a highly competitive sports, high school, and college background, for me it simply outlines my belief that every minute of every day I try to make decisions in a way that will elevate not only my professional but personal life. There is never a moment or opportunity to settle. High gear is having the willingness to be my personal best no matter what the outcome is. High gear is a way of thinking that not only impacts my accomplishments, but drives me to push to the next level of my business and personal goals.

As a senior at TCU, I realize that being selected to be part of the 30 Next Generation Leadership Program (NGLP) early in my college career provided the mentorship and knowledge to realize that your best cannot be compared or equated to your peers'. We each have specific qualities and characteristics that set us apart and drive our ambitions and personal achievements. High gear provides the clutch that shifts us from the ordinary to the extraordinary. It allows our achievements and doubts to serve us and to allow us to grow to our potential and realize not only our accomplishments, but also the value in our doubts and failures.

Looking at these accomplishments, I realize there is a common thread. High gear means that not only can I accomplish my goals as a young, female professional, but I can do it on my terms. My greatest compliment came from a professor when I was really struggling with the program. His simple compliment to a group of my peers was that I am the most "sincere dedicated person" he has ever met.

That statement alone propelled me into high gear. It allowed me to realize that as imperfect as I might think I am in comparison to an outrageously talented group of students in the BNSF NGLP program and Neeley Business School, my best effort and drive is what matters. Striving to work my absolute hardest at whatever I may do is what high gear means to me. It not only portrays my own personal beliefs and talents, but it comes with the experience of doubt and failure. I have worked throughout college and currently have three jobs, which at times can be very challenging. At some points, I felt like I was doing poorly in every aspect of college and my professional world. However, if it wasn't for the hard lessons I learned and failures I experienced, I wouldn't have grown to be to where I am today.

Time management is not the only thing that has been embedded into my brain after being in high gear. At times I feel like I am going 100 miles a minute while everyone else is going in slow motion, but in actuality, I can't compare myself to others. If I have learned anything from my life always in high gear, it's to focus on yourself and your own growth. Don't get involved in petty competition, and don't run a one-woman show. But create and grow an exceptional team. Surrounding yourself with hard-working, dedicated people is vital. There were many times that someone on my team had to pick me up and put me back together. There are times when you won't be able to go 100 miles a minute, and you will need those people to support you.

High gear doesn't mean you do whatever you can to succeed and get to the top in the fastest way possible. It means taking advantage of every single opportunity life gives you, and surrounding yourself with people who want the same thing.

The idea of high gear acts as a setting in my life. It provides me a system of checks-and-balances that allows me to set the bar a little higher than my normal comfort level. High gear is a progression. It starts slow with a simple idea and drives the end product through a series of escalations toward an end goal. Each gear lets me escalate my thoughts and goals in an effort to push me to the next level, whether personal or professional. This shift is imperative for the young professional. It allows me to feel that I am not only prepared but can embrace the challenges of being a young, professional woman. High gear has provided an acceleration of my game plan and gives me a foundation. It is where I start, and where I work from each and every day. High gear is the drive and daily ambition in my world.

Sarah Womack, Graduate, Rhodes College

Being high gear can mean various things. We all have our own unique journey to reach our own version. For me, it began when I decided to attend Rhodes College. I made this decision on a few key criteria. I knew it would challenge me and prepare me for a path I wanted to take. At Rhodes, I played women's basketball, took a leadership role in my sorority, and gained professional experience in an incredible internship at St. Jude Children's Research Hospital. Following graduation, I was accepted to an MBA graduate program. All of my hard work led me to a job offer and acceptance post graduation. However, as life and business goes, there was an unexpected shift in plans due to unforeseen market developments. When I found myself confronted by a daunting obstacle, I was able to pull myself together and get back out and search for my next opportunity where I was thrilled to meet Amy Howell, a fellow Rhodes graduate. I was given the opportunity to learn from her during my "changing of gears" and have continued on my path to reach high gear.

As unique as all our journeys to high gear can be, I have begun to see similarities in the stories I have heard. During my time with Amy Howell and from my experiences thus far in life, I have come to find that being high gear means a few things:

Don't be afraid to fail. You can't reach high gear without trying to do things you have never done before. No matter how much education or experience you have, we all will undoubtedly encounter something that challenges us. Sometimes this means you might get it wrong, but no one gets better by playing it safe.

Learn constantly. No matter where you went to school, how many degrees you have, or how long you have been working, there is always more to learn. Being high gear means having a curious and open mind and constantly learning. Reach out to as many people as you can. Learning from others' mistakes rather than making all your own allows for a shorter learning curve.

Build relationships. Part of your ability to be high gear is having the support system on the days that your goals seem out of reach. You can't be high gear alone. Part of building relationships is participating in the support system needed for others.

CHAPTER 2

Your Digital Footprint Starts Early

"You're known by the company you ~~keep~~ tweet!"

AESOP'S FABLE

In our new normal, we are living with a technological reality: "You are who Google says you are." It's hard to believe that Steve Jobs introduced the iPhone in June of 2007—only eight short years ago—and in May 2014 it surpassed its 500 millionth unit sold. Even for adults, it's hard to remember life without a digital device. For our children and grandchildren, digital access provides amazing opportunities with equally amazing access to reputational destruction.

Today's babies are the first humans in history to have their digital imprint begin before they take their first breath. And it's a digital story they inherit, with no editing control during the early years.

We live in a digital, global world where news is 24/7, and you have more technology in your pocket than the White House had 20 years ago. When your parents were your age, they had three ways to communicate: in person, by phone, and by USPS mail. That's it.

It can be difficult for parents or professors to adapt to these new technologies, but it's imperative that they keep pace with you. *Students in High Gear* also applies to adult learners and virtual learners who comprise a significant portion of the 21 million students in college. You don't have the luxury of making mistakes—your bad choices will be captured on Twitter or YouTube for the world to see.

Learn now to leverage this new media and be prepared for the reality that your digital footprint is indelible and eternal.

AMY

Students need to ask themselves this question: What does my digital footprint say about me? Colleges, recruiters, employers, coaches—they are all looking at your digital footprint. Make sure yours is clean enough to get hired, recruited for a scholarship, or considered for an internship.

> **If you don't want to see it on the front page of a newspaper, don't post it. If your mother or your preacher would see it and be embarrassed, don't post it.**

If you have questionable items in your streams, clean them up. Go through your Instagram photos, and look at each one to make sure you are comfortable with what you've shared. Don't follow or accept followers who don't share your values. Do you know who would screenshot something and repost it? Don't follow them, and limit what they see. Don't feel the need to share personal information like your home address, where your Dad works, and what your little sister is doing.

Don't Snapchat at all hours of the night—you need sleep, and if you expect a high gear life, you don't want to crash and burn in college. Don't use profanity or engage in any way with posting or sharing nudity. Don't post anything harmful or detrimental to yourself or others. What you post now matters. You can't assume that you can take it back. Posting online on **any** site is three things: **permanent, global,** and **discoverable** in a court of law. Facebook, Twitter, Instagram, LinkedIn, YouTube, and Pinterest all have Law Enforcement Guidelines and civil subpoena processes.

As an employer of younger adults in their 20s, I have watched online discussions and made the decision *not* to interview someone based on how they post and what they say.

I recently reviewed the resume of a new college graduate who was job hunting. As a Twitter user, I decided to look her up on Twitter. Her resume said one thing and her tweets quite the opposite. I moved on to the next resume. What you say on social media matters. It can prevent you from opportunities that you might not even know about.

Another candidate I considered interviewing kept tweeting that she was "living for the weekend" and "Is it 5:00 yet?"—not career-enhancing tweets in my opinion. My assumption based on her posts is that she doesn't value her job and isn't smart enough to keep her thoughts about work to herself. Many young adults wrongly believe that employers and parents aren't using social media. Oh, what a bad assumption to make.

In today's business climate of limited resources and productivity demands, students cannot afford to be negligent on social media. Further, students who graduate and have already built their fan base online may be more attractive to potential employers. Don't wait until you graduate from college to build your connections online. Do it while you are in college. Start making connections on LinkedIn and Twitter with people you admire or might want to work for.

High gear students use social media tools to reflect a strong work ethic. Businesses are seeking college graduates who understand that success isn't delivered on a silver platter but is hard earned. If you can showcase strong values and ethics across your social platforms and build your base before you graduate, you are showing employers that you are ahead of the curve—that you understand the importance of having a digital strategy and how to use it.

Additionally, your digital footprint should show productive content. Blogging is a great way to display your work and connect with influencers. Share good news about innovative ideas. Tweeting links to articles you may find in top industry publications would be a great strategy, and make sure you actually read them. View these tools as ways to build your brand online. Even if you don't have a job yet, you still are developing a personal brand. Claim your space on the social sites. Create a profile and be consistent across the platforms. High gear students understand the power of social tools and can use them for business success.

I have written often about this on my blog. For more on these topics, you can visit www.howell-marketing.com, and you can also find more information in Chapter 9 of *Women in High Gear* on Amazon.

Is your goal to start your own business someday? Use your skills to become an entrepreneur. Seek out and connect with leaders in that space. Watch what they post, and read what they are saying on blogs. Twitter and LinkedIn are excellent social tools for researching people and companies. Studies show that students spend too much time on YouTube. Your time would be better spent understanding and unlocking the power of LinkedIn. Use these online tools to further your ambition and fuel your passions. You can meet incredible contacts online who can help you and who can hire you for that matter.

Social media is not there to tell everyone what you are eating and how drunk someone got Friday night. Rather, social media is a path to showing the world how you can add value. Social media gives you a huge stage. How will you act on it? What will you say? Will other people follow you and respect you? Can you connect with influential people, and can you convince them to help you or hire you?

Harness the power of social media to your advantage, and use it as a strategic way to grow and find paths to success. We tell our clients it's important to have a strategy for using social tools. That would also apply to you as an individual. Social media gives you the powerful opportunity to engage with thought leaders across the world without having to get on an airplane. Meaningful connections are at your fingertips. If you are interested in engineering, get on Twitter and search the hashtags #Engineering, #Engineer, and #Jobs.

Listen to what influential business people are saying and note who they are. Watch what they post and learn from them. If you are in Journalism and you want to intern with a PR firm, get on Twitter and start searching hashtags like #PR, #Journalism, #MediaChat, and #BlogChat and then engage with real people behind those Twitter handles. How? Pick up the phone and call them.

Examples are endless and contacts are even more endless. People are out there looking at you and for you. Make it count. The true ROI of social media is connecting to people in-person who can help you. While not everyone is in a position to hire you, they are in a position to refer you to someone who can advance your career.

Lauren King, Senior, Texas Christian University

A digital footprint is all of the information online about an individual either posted by that person or others intentionally or unintentionally. You create your digital footprint through all your online actions, activities, and communication. Just as you are able to Google yourself and find information about yourself, college administration offices, professors, and employers can easily do the same.

Now you may be asking, "How can I manage my own digital footprint and ensure that these horrible things do not happen to me?" Great question! I am not suggesting to completely hide from the Internet forever. I am recommending to be the person you want to be both offline and online. Post achievements, articles, and other things you are proud of. I have learned how to do this successfully over the years. Many parents and professors have drilled us hard on this subject. I have learned that you must monitor your personal sites and social media accounts from Day 1.

ANNE

Managing your online reputation begins in elementary school or earlier and continues the rest of your life. The good news is that social media allows you to tell your story and be found online. The bad news is that social media allows you to tell your story and be found online. You control the keys to your cyber kingdom.

My daughter-in-law is in her 20s and teaches fourth grade. Everyday she helps her students understand Digital Citizenship. "As we stress 21st-century learning, we use digital standards to help guide our young students into technology integration," Mallary Gallaher says.

"Rather than fight this technology sweep, schools are realizing that we need to equip this generation with the knowledge of how to appropriately and properly interact with the digital world. Twenty-six of my 27 students bring their own Internet-capable device to school every day. It may sit in their backpacks, but they have it with them. We use apps for learning, like Kahoot, a quiz-like website where a teacher inputs review questions and students use their devices to buzz in their vote and compete against classmates for review points. Middle-school students use their devices for research and apps for educational purposes," she shares.

The social media channel of choice for her elementary students is Instagram. "Facebook doesn't exist to this younger generation." Part of the Digital Citizenship creed that she teaches her students is to "Advocate and practice safe, legal, and responsible use of information and technology. Demonstrate personal responsibility for lifelong learning." If today's fourth graders can master digital responsibility, their paths to high gear will be much smoother and their reputations much safer.

Begin today to align your high gear goals with your social media profiles. You may be reading this as a high school junior and think it doesn't apply to you yet. Just as every course grade matters in senior high school, every tweet/text/email/Snapchat/Instagram/DM, and

Facebook post matters, too. You may think that an app like Snapchat (created by three Stanford University students in 2011) is the safest to use because your message self-destructs in 1–10 seconds; but remember, every social media application has a server. If you don't want to be quoted as saying it, or recognized in an inappropriate photo for public view, don't Snapchat it.

Your shared content forms a digital composite of who you really are. Recruiters not only visit your social media profiles, they check out who you tweet and engage with. What company do you keep online, so to speak? If you're a college graduate, what groups do you belong to on LinkedIn? What chats do you participate in? These friends and influencers become your digital references. Does your online brand match up with your on-paper brand?

Because Amy and I work in public relations and are professional communicators, we create content every day for companies both big and small—entertainment companies, entertainers, publicly traded corporations, financial institutions, and privately held firms. Just like students' tweets, corporate tweets define the corporation. Every business has a digital tattoo as well. And the damage to a business reputation can be equally devastating. Warren Buffett, one of the world's most successful investors and the second richest man on the planet said, "It takes 20 years to build a reputation and five minutes to ruin it. If you think about that, you'll do things differently."

I am surprised at the volume of personal health information I see shared in Facebook feeds and on Twitter from young people. Guard your health information privacy, and do not share your diagnoses, your ER visits, your family's hospitalizations, your prescription medicines, or your emotional stressors. All content posted on Twitter is archived on Google and preserved by the U.S. Library of Congress. Do you really want insurance companies and potential employers to know this information? There are a few extenuating circumstances to this rule, and Amy will write about this in another book.

Five years from now, when you're newly married, do you really want to see your "relationship rant" when a boyfriend or girlfriend ditched you? Seek the wise counsel of a trusted friend, parent, teacher, or pastor to share personal information with, not your online community. Your social media disgorge can seriously hamper your career opportunities.

Some simple steps to creating a positive digital tattoo begin with removing any bad language. Use a good picture of yourself in a professional setting as your profile picture. And use the same picture across every channel as you begin to build your personal brand.

Don't post pictures of yourself in bathing suits, and don't be fooled that because everyone else in college does it that it's okay. Don't use inappropriate hashtags on Instagram, don't be snarky, and don't use profile pictures featuring you with another person.

Imagine that every tweet, post, and picture is a potential conversation-starter at your job interview. If it would embarrass you to see it on a Powerpoint slide, don't post it.

If you Google "fired over a tweet," you'll see 53.3 million results of social media content that got people fired. You don't want to end up in this Search result.

The popular saying found in Aesop's Fable that "You're known by the company you keep" now means "You're known by the company you tweet." Who do you engage with online? Set high gear goals to meet influencers in the career path you're choosing. With a little strategy and smart thinking, you can bypass gatekeepers and start to build college connections and business relationships with people in your industry long before you graduate. An easy place to begin is by attending digital conferences or events at your college or in your hometown.

Our Harrisburg Social Media Club hosts monthly events that are open to anyone interested in meeting and learning with us, and they are always held at a business. Executives, managers, social media professionals, and entrepreneurs fill the room to talk about new tools to drive business success.

We love to see students attending, and it's a perfect forum to begin a personal brand by taking a few pictures with business people and posting them using the group's hashtag. Our annual digital conference titled Social Media at Work (#SMatWork15) has discounted student rates, and we look for every opportunity to welcome young learners into the group.

CHAPTER 3

The Road to College: High Gear High School

"Always be a first-rate version of yourself,
instead of a second-rate version of somebody else."

JUDY GARLAND

For 12 years, the activity that will consume the largest chunk of your day is school. According to the U.S. Bureau of Labor Statistics Time Use Study (www.bls.gov), students spend 6.6 hours every weekday in a classroom. They spend 8.7 hours sleeping, and 3.6 hours each day socializing, relaxing, and in leisure time. We talked earlier about one of the world's most prized non-renewable resources—your time. Spend it wisely, and you'll be far ahead of your peers.

In high school, start to think about where you want to be in five years, 10 years, and 20 years. Some of your most powerful allies during high school are your teachers, and they can open many doors for you. Ask them for advice on study habits, test-taking, and college and career choices. They are the ones who will be writing your college recommendations, your job references, and introducing you to college admissions officers.

AMY

Hutchison School in Memphis, Tennessee, is a school in high gear. When our first book came out, they invited me to speak to their seniors, and I was impressed by the girls who bought the book and read it. Additionally, Hutchison has expressed a passion for leadership and is producing high gear young women who are moving into high gear college experiences. Here are some stories from the faculty and students.

Kathryn Jasper, Leads Director, Hutchison School, Memphis, Tennessee

You can (and should) be high gear in high school. As Hutchison Leads Director, I work closely with girls in grades 9–12 to develop their leadership ability. At Hutchison School, an independent school for girls grades Pre-K–12 in Memphis, Tennessee, we are developing a girl's mind, body, and spirit. The co-curricular leadership opportunities that partner with and complement the classroom academic experience include service learning, internships, public policy field lessons, global travel, and more. In working with all girls in the upper school, the core value of Hutchison Leads focuses on the belief that everyone is a leader in her own particular way. The first step in our program is for all freshmen to spend a quarter in a seminar being introspective and learning about their own leadership style. As the girls grow through the program, they are encouraged to explore and identify their passion and purpose. As high schoolers, the girls are given the autonomy to implement their own projects and ideas. Adults advise and facilitate, mentoring the girls as they grow and develop.

For example, our editors of the print newspaper decided they wanted to go online and pair the print paper with an online edition. The newspaper advisor encouraged them to research the options and create a proposal for the change. The editors took this proposal to school leadership, who supported the endeavor. The girls then spent a semester working with school leaders to design a website and create a style guide for an online newspaper. The end result launched this past fall with interactive polls, video reporting, and a wider array of stories that an online platform allows. These editors saw their dream from inception to reality, which was rewarding in itself, but the real treasure appears behind the scenes—the editors learned about project management, onboarding stakeholders, and management. This experience exemplifies high gear in high school at Hutchison School—these editors truly are high gear women.

So how can you be high gear as well? The same blueprint that we use in our program with our girls can be implemented on an individual level. Focus on identifying your personal strengths, knowing that leadership manifests itself in many different forms and that it takes all sorts of talents to be successful. You can identify personal strengths by thinking about times you succeeded, whether it be on a project, in a group, or in a leadership capacity. You can also spend time completing personality inventories. These are helpful in thinking through not only your strengths but also your blind spots or the areas of your personality that you may need to work on.

After spending time being introspective, identify your passion and follow it. That may be through opportunities at school or in the community. Seek mentors that share your passion, learn from their experiences, and outline your goals. Most importantly, do not let your age restrict your passion. High school students can make a large impact. Lastly, do not forget to be reflective upon completion of your experience. One of the biggest traits of being high gear is learning and growing with each step.

Gabi Stein, Senior, Hutchison School, Memphis, Tennessee

After contemplating the meaning of acting in high gear, I realized two leading principles I have been following throughout the past four years.

Principle 1: Get involved in every aspect of the community where you live, but more importantly, the school where you spend more time than your home. This idea can be applied to a 9–12 school or a K–12 school. My school starts with a two-year-old program and goes until 12th grade. I have volunteered the past four summers in Early Childhood to mold the next generation of Hutchison scholars: Memphis-lovers, STEM-questioners, and lifelong learners. During my sophomore year in high school, I became involved with Rogers Scholars, an organization at my school that brings forth a multitude of Memphis-based issues. As a group, we traveled to Overton Park to explore the issues related to conserving Memphis's Old Forest that contains some of the oldest trees in Memphis, and how the zoo improves our economy. Following, we toured the new Civil Rights Museum. Next, we toured the STAX museum and then met and discussed issues with teens our age at the charter school connected to the museum. The last field trip of the semester was at the Memphis Farmers Market to learn about urban farming. Being a part of my community has provided me with more opportunities and instilled in me a desire to make a connection with every community I encounter.

Principle 2: Find your passions, all of them. Do not limit them. Then, try to weave them together. I fortuitously discovered journalism my sophomore year after a scheduling error. It was thrilling to work under a deadline to create pieces of writing the whole school would read and finding the perfect layout to configure every article, picture, and byline together. Now, somewhere in my high school career, feminism popped into my life. It was not handed to me like journalism, but we found each other. I confidently fight and support for equal rights among genders. Finally, STEM (science, technology, engineering, and math) has always been important to me. I have taken the most challenging classes, but I wanted more. I filled my extra time with these subjects as well. The most interesting was flipping the situation. I became the educator. I took the opportunity to create an interactive iBook chapter at St. Jude Children's Research Hospital, because I want to make every child interested in STEM. I was also able to combine the knowledge I have gained from the classroom with the information I learned from the fellowship, such as Bloom's taxonomy, to create a more well-rounded curriculum for St. Jude's separate biology iBook. The iBook chapter I created consists of a case study in which students learn about diagnosis, cells, and leukemia. The iBook utilizes interactive pictures that show the difference between cancerous and noncancerous cells, along with definitions that zoom to points on the images to gather a clearer understanding. Thus, I am pushing the envelope of service by modernizing curriculum and making biology more accessible to students. Creating, gaining, and sharing knowledge is my long-term desire. As I progress toward this goal, I make sure to challenge myself every day because a day without learning is a day wasted.

Ivy Wagerman, Senior, Hutchison School, Memphis, Tennessee

To me, high gear means taking full advantage of every opportunity that comes your way. Some of these opportunities may come easily but others are more challenging to grasp, which only makes them that much more rewarding. Looking back, even from a young age, I would consider myself to be in high gear, plunging head first into opportunities to experience new things. I believe high gear is about learning from new experiences.

The 15 years I spent at Hutchison School encouraged me to be high gear inside and outside of the classroom. Through leadership positions, teamwork, and challenges, I have learned that experiences outside of the classroom are equally, if not more, valuable than any lesson learned in the classroom or textbook. I have taken full advantage of all that Hutchison has to offer, but I learned the most from my four years serving as an elected officer for the class of 2015 and my involvement in Hutchison Leads. As an officer, my leadership, organization, communication, and marketing skills flourished and grew. Eager for more opportunity for growth, I worked with the amazing Hutchison Leads team to help find a summer internship that would focus on some of these skills that I had enjoyed so much. After reaching out to many of my own contacts, Mrs. Jasper, the coordinator of Hutchison Leads, came to me with a great opportunity to intern at Howell Marketing Strategies. Even though this name was unfamiliar to me at the time, I immediately said yes to such a new and exciting experience.

From the first moments of my internship I was encouraged to be in high gear. Throughout my internship, I worked closely with each team member to learn more about their roles, and quickly got involved by completing everyday tasks. Just from being in the office with Mrs. Washburn, Client Services Manager, I learned about the importance of communication and keeping up with the news of all markets that clients are placed in. I learned more about how social media has changed the business of marketing and the importance of presence on social media. I followed the lead of the Social Media Coordinator by composing posts for a variety of clients to share on their social media sites for their followers. I loved seeing the different tasks of each person in the office and how each of their skills worked together to give clients the best service.

I was immediately encouraged by Mrs. Howell to be in high gear by being included in every aspect of her job and the realm of marketing. I was able to attend client meetings and get a hands-on experience on what client relations are like and doing follow-up research or posting. I was even able to see Mrs. Howell in action, promoting *Women in High Gear*, and how she seamlessly related it to her life. Since I was so encouraged to be in high gear, I learned more than just about marketing from my internship.

As I move forward and attend the University of Mississippi after graduating from Hutchison, I will continue to be in high gear by taking advantage of all opportunities I am faced with, learning from challenging experiences, and keeping in touch with the many people that have had a positive role in my journey so far.

I can always attribute my high gear attitude to the encouragement of Hutchison Leads and Mrs. Howell.

Tara Lore, Senior, Texas Christian University

The secret to success is not about being the busiest person. It is about finding something that truly makes you feel alive. When you find your passion, you will see that work ceases to be tedious or boring, because when you love what you do you never work a day in your life. Once you find your passion, success will follow. I urge high school students to stop joining organizations and taking on more activities. The stress that follows a busy life only creates wrinkles. Instead, take a moment to notice the people around you, build real relationships, create connections, and focus your energy on finding the one thing you are the best at.

We realize that some students like Gabi and Ivy are in private high schools which afford them many advantages. Others struggle to graduate from high school in average or poor economic conditions. However, great work is being done across this country by generous philanthropies like the Bill & Melinda Gates Foundation and the Hyde Foundation (Memphis) to further advantages for as many as possible when it comes to education being a priority in our country.

Our economic stability and future depend on a well-educated, skilled workforce. We also believe America's future depends on having graduates who passionately pursue their high gear in all aspects of life. Seeking high gear in high school is critical because it lays the groundwork for where you go to college, graduate school, law or medical school. Or you may opt for a degree from a technical school or trade school. Our world needs all types of students working in high gear no matter what level or profession they select. The key is finding a high gear career that you are passionate about, good at, and where you can excel, and earn a living.

High gear high school means you pay attention to what you excel at, get involved, and do extra-curricular work that matters and that demonstrates what you are passionate about. If you can communicate why you chose certain activities with passion and show how you helped make a difference, you will have an advantage. If you take aptitude tests and know what your strengths are, you will have an advantage. There are plenty of books written for students on how to get into college, so we are not writing about that. Rather, we are sharing tips for reaching your high gear in high school and in college in order that you are marketable to potential employers after college.

One challenge we have as a society is this continuous bar-raising for all students to excel at everything. That isn't realistic, and we are kidding ourselves if we think having all "outstanding and excellent" students is the goal. Creating a bunch of identical, perfect, straight-A-at-everything students is not the answer. The goal should be equipping students with what they need to learn, teaching them how to study, and how to uniquely share their passion and stories in an increasingly complex world, so that they may apply it productively in the workforce. And in the end, if our students cannot find jobs, they cannot earn a living, and they won't have the resources or time to give back to the community. The most successful businesspeople generously give back to the communities in which they built their success.

High gear is about finding what you're good at so you can get a job that leads to a career that you are passionate about. "Following your dream" is for dreamers, and dreaming alone is not a strategy. Instead, we are advocates of finding your passion—both in and out of the classroom—and applying it successfully through hard work and actions.

My daughter Abby is in high school at St. Benedict at Auburndale Catholic High, and recently I had the honor of speaking about high gear to the faculty at the school. This opportunity arose as a direct result of publishing our first book. During my talk, I mentioned that we were in the midst of writing this book, and I asked the principal if she would like to contribute, as we believe high gear starts young! SBA is another Memphis high gear high school, and—although new to us—I can tell you that Abby is thriving and achieving high gear there. Here are Ms. Sondra Morris' words of wisdom from her perspective at SBA:

I have the privilege of serving as the Principal at St. Benedict at Auburndale Catholic High School in Cordova, Tennessee. I am also a wife and mother of five. My days are filled with energetic teenagers, and I can honestly say, most days do not follow my To-Do list, but I believe that is an integral part of any educator's day.

We educators could not do our part if it were not for the first educators of each child, their parents. Preparing students for life after high school is a team effort and an ongoing challenge—not an overnight exercise.

We want our students to excel in all aspects of life, and we also want them to continue to grow and mature in their daily walk of life. We all want our students to be accepted not only to a college, but to the college of their choice. Furthermore, we want our students to be successful in their chosen school.

Preparing our students for the next phase of their lives is a huge responsibility. I'm blessed to be surrounded with a faculty and staff that wants nothing but the best possible performance from each student. What does that mean to the faculty/staff member? Among many things, it means that each one must continue to challenge not just their students, but also themselves. Our faculty has done just that. They have embraced all of the wonders of technology while still incorporating the best traditional teaching strategies and assessment methods in order to give our students the foundation they need to achieve excellence wherever they go.

Students in high gear—they take advantage of the educational opportunities offered to them; they learn more from their mistakes than their successes; they take responsibility for their own lifelong learning; and they are brave in taking risks that enhance their own growth. More importantly, these students are just as concerned about the world around them as they are about their personal achievements. They are the ones that realize that service and concern for our community, our country, and our world makes the successes we earn even more meaningful.

It is my fortune to witness these high gear students grow into responsible citizens and productive individuals. I am honored to be a part of every SBA student's academic life and watch with anticipation what the future holds for each one.

ANNE

The choices you make in high school can change the course of your life; and the friends you choose in high school can do the same. An important fact to remember during these exciting and sometimes tumultuous years is from A.A. Milne: "You are braver than you believe, stronger than you seem, and smarter than you think." As someone who has 35 years of life experience after high school, I can tell you that it's the truth.

My husband has been a high school chemistry teacher for 34 years. He sets a high bar for his students knowing that if they do their part and study hard, they'll reach a higher gear than they ever imagined.

What's the biggest change he's observed in more than 30 years in the classroom? "Kids are much more compassionate and respectful now compared to when I was in school and when I first began teaching," he told me. "Aside from the titanic shifts in technology, parental interaction has changed and not always for the betterment of the student. There are parents who will meet with teachers, not to understand how we can help their son or daughter master a concept or equation, but to defend them in wrongdoing. That was unheard of when I was in high school."

There are 1,300 students in his high school and his laser-focus hasn't changed since he began teaching: "I have a clear goal to prepare them for college. I can't help them adjust socially, but I sure can help them understand the material and give them one less hurdle to leap in their college transition." The reality is that your high school teachers are a tremendous resource in preparing you for college, in helping you find your high gear, and in holding you accountable for high standards of learning.

Not one student has ever told my husband that they wished they hadn't worked so hard in his class. Or that they were too prepared for college. On the contrary, scores have returned to school over the years to thank him for his passion for teaching chemistry.

When they felt like giving up, he encouraged them. When they thought they wouldn't pass Chem II, he stayed after class to tutor them. When they needed a reference for an after-school job, he knew them well enough to write it. When they went on to medical school or engineering school or a trade school, they thanked him for making sure they had the best tools to succeed.

"It really isn't about chemistry, it's about being assigned a task and completing the task set before you. Maybe 5% of my students will become chemists, but whether they make a Big Mac or create the next breakthrough cancer drug, they need to be able to listen, use critical thinking skills, and complete the task I assign them. I had a student tell me recently, 'You really take it personally when I don't complete my homework.' Yes, I do," says Corey Gallaher.

A chem student this spring handed my husband a poem she wrote to show her appreciation for his deep desire to see all his students reach high gear: "Thank you for being such a great teacher! You helped me get back into the groove of loving to learn, and wanting As in all my classes! I absolutely loved your class, surprisingly fence-posting showed up in calculus. Keep being awesome!"

In high school, seek out a mentor-teacher. Someone you can relate to, who will be an encourager and advocate for you. This might also be a youth pastor, a parent, a coach, or a Scout leader. Keep an open line of communication with as many adults as possible, and ask for their advice and support. Teachers are your first line of defense in preparing for college, so tap into their higher-ed connections and chart a path to college success together.

"Be active in different groups," says my oldest son Joshua who graduated with a marketing degree from Penn State University. "Join and lead clubs. Try elective classes that will introduce you to a whole new group of people. I wish I would have taken electives like photography. If you're an athlete, attend the musicals. If you're in the choir, attend the wrestling matches. Stretch yourself to meet new people. And try to make a difference in every activity and class you're a part of. I started a mowing business when I was in high school, and I was able to buy my own pickup truck when I was 16. I was also able to include that on my college application and it sends a strong signal about your work ethic."

Many high school students are working part-time, and this is valuable for time management skills and financial literacy. When you list any work experience on a job application or college application, it demonstrates responsibility and self-discipline as well as teamwork. If you're in Scouts, stay in Scouts. Learning life skills and leadership training in the Boy Scouts or Girl Scouts is one of the fastest ways to reach a high gear in college. These character traits will help you advance more quickly in college and can be a powerful negotiating edge when you start your career.

CHAPTER 4

Your Father's Resume Is Dead

*"Far and away the best prize that life offers
is the chance to work hard at work worth doing."*

THEODORE ROOSEVELT

Before you get the "chance to work hard at work worth doing," you'll need to present your qualifications—your personal brand— to an employer. We called them resumes. Today's recruiters and job seekers call them Google Searches. A college admissions officer might read your Twitter bio to get a snapshot of who you are, or listen to a YouTube video you're tagged in. Will your digital resume reinforce all the achievements you've included in your paper resume?

Resumes have evolved over time and are now reinvented in digital formats. Once typed on a typewriter and printed on a quality stock paper, resumes were then mailed to their destination. Back in the day, the printed resume was really the only shred of evidence that a person was who she or he said they were. What we know as job hunting and resume writing has morphed into a booming online, robust recruiting revolution. Are you joining that conversation as a college student? Are you spending time watching these online phenomenons like LinkedIn? In the 80s and 90s, graduates secured jobs because their Dads—and Moms too, but mostly the Dads— connected them to influential people that could hire them or direct them to those who could. While this still happens (more on this in Chapter 9: Dot-Connecting and Why You Must Master It) and students need to leverage their parents' connections, the world is much more competitive and it takes more than a connection to land a job.

The difference between today and the late 80s is that you can now connect with these influencers yourself, and more importantly, you have powerful information at your fingertips. A huge advantage! We mentioned earlier that your "digital tattoo" is being formed at an early age. This now becomes part of your online DNA. What people say about you, who you hang out with online—all of this comprises your resume. How will you use it? Here are some of our back stories and some of our digital advice we tell students and graduates seeking jobs in this competitive global job market.

AMY

Resumes in the 80s were our calling cards. Today, they are conversation starters. Back then resumes were the only way to showcase what we had done, and they were limited to one or two pages. There was no Internet or computers, so mailing our resumes was how we job searched. Imagine mailing a resume and waiting the two to four days it took for someone to get it. And then, often times it sat unopened somewhere in a mailroom in the basement. It's a wonder people even got jobs back then.

Fast forward to today's instant everything world, and although the resume is still relevant, it is electronic in format and the main method of distribution in business is email. Although the format and distribution methods have changed, the importance of the content on the resume has not. It is important to start building a resume in high school. My son Bryan is beginning his freshman year at the University of Memphis. As I write this, we have mastered the process of college applications and resume building. The key for students is that it all adds up and works together.

Every job, award, and achievement you master is captured on your digital resume. But again, a resume today is only a conversation starter. What you must do is put compelling content on the resume that gets noticed and after that, you must communicate face to face, eye to eye, *persuasively*. In this age of texting constantly, students must master the fine art of communication in real life. If you have not learned and practiced interviewing skills, get to it! Find help and look to people you know in the business world to help you.

LinkedIn has a host of resume templates you can use to format a resume. You can change it to best match up opportunities focusing on key strengths and skills. Using LinkedIn to update your bio and add key accomplishments is a great way to produce a resume. And it is a great place to record all of your accomplishments. As you progress through schooling and a career, you tend to forget what you have done. Part of my continuing high gear has been to archive my jobs and accomplishments on LinkedIn. When I am asked to speak, I send my LinkedIn bio to whomever introduces me. Additionally, people who search for me can see what I do and what I have accomplished over the past 25 years of my career.

As far as content goes, students need to do research on companies they would like to approach for work. What does the company do? Is it publicly held? What information is accessible online about this company? How does this company make money? What is the company's value statement? Who is on its Board of Directors? What does the press say about this company? Answering these questions and doing research is critical to how you write your resume. For example, even using a font style on your resume that matches the corporate brand identity of a company you want to engage with would be smart. You force the recruiter to ask, "Is this a coincidence or is this candidate sending us a deliberate and positive message that says I understand you, have studied you, and want to work with you.'"

Here are my tips for resumes for college students:
1. Study who you are sending your resume to. Follow them online, and be sure you know a lot about them before you

tailor your resume. If you find that they support the arts, for example, and you have helped raise money for an arts organization, make sure you put that in a cover letter and certainly use it in a conversation later. Be deliberate. Be strategic.

2. Write a cover letter. No exceptions. Make sure it is well written, grammatically correct, and free of errors. Make sure it is interesting and contains several reasons why I should care about you. Make sure you use the proper name and title of the recipient and be gracious and thankful for the consideration. Manners matter. Include something interesting you've read about the person you're submitting to. I'm always appreciative of students who have taken time to learn something about me and mention it. Small details are big when it comes to job hunting.

3. List jobs in chronological order and be clear on dates. This is one of the biggest and most careless errors I find on college graduates' resumes. Employers are looking for those who can submit an error-free resume.

4. Ask someone to review, critique, and help you write your resume if you don't know how. The Internet is also a great resource and you should use as many tools as possible.

5. Include civic, charitable, and leadership activities you have participated in. Employers want to see well-rounded students who have done more than just graduate with a good GPA.

6. Entertain a creative resume (I received a video resume recently), but don't go crazy with it. It is fine to think outside of the box, but not too much. You want your resume to get you in the door for a first meeting or phone call. If you go too far, it might be a risk that you get passed over because you are too creative. It also depends on what industry you are looking at. If you send a video to a law firm, I'm fairly sure

you won't get a call; however, advertising agencies love that type of creativity. Again, know your target.

7. Don't send a resume to a website and think that is all you have to do! You must follow up and talk to real people. Be persistent and apply for as many jobs as you can.

8. Less is more. Be brief, be bright, and limit it to one page if you can.

9. If you include references, make certain you let them know and have their prior approval. There is nothing worse for a candidate than a reference being caught off guard.

Patti Clauss is a dear friend. She is vice president, Global Talent Acquisition for Williams Sonoma Inc. and shares her insights. She searches the globe for talent for a living.

Dear Students:

I am vice president of Global Talent Acquisition for Williams Sonoma Inc. (WSI). WSI is a multi-channel specialty retailer of high-quality products for the home. I have been with WSI for almost 13 years and have been a recruiter, talent scout, researcher of people, and connector for almost 30 years. I grew up in a small town in Arkansas to parents who were educators and farmers. I was taught to work hard both physically and mentally. I have a BA in English and am a lover of words, in any form.

It made perfect sense when my high gear friend and colleague Amy Howell asked me to share my views on the importance of communication in a career search in her second book, *Students in High Gear.* I hope you find these next few paragraphs helpful in your quest for success both personally and professionally.

At every phase of a career you must be curious, ask questions, and discover. There is power in learning and interacting with others. When I say the word communication, what is the first reaction you have? Do you reach for your phone (perhaps you are reading this on your mobile device or tablet?) to see if you have a text message, a new Twitter follower, perhaps a Like on Instagram? Communication today is done through a variety of means. It is important for us who are established in our careers to help students realize the power of verbal and written (full sentences) communication.

As I mentioned, I am a communicator; some call me a connector, which is also true. To be a connector, I must first be a communicator, and a strong one at that. I speak to people all across the globe on a daily basis. I do this through every means possible: phone, email, Twitter, blogs, Instagram, and Facebook. You name it; I use it. But the art I see fading daily is the Art of Professional Communication. Communication where you can truly be "felt," where your passion can come through. There are two main ways for that to happen and for a true understanding of the message you are trying to convey: First is verbal communication. Remember, where you actually speak one-on-one to another human being? This can certainly be scary, yes, but if we can stop hiding behind a device, great things will happen. Secondly, is the written word. Not abbreviations, not emojis, but beautiful words well written, well presented, and conveyed. These are the ways of communicating that will land you that acceptance into the college about which you have been dreaming, as well as communication that will land you that first real job after graduation.

You researched your school online, even found and applied for your first job online, but to be the one noticed you have to be able to convey who you are and why you should be the one selected rather than the 100s perhaps 1,000s of others. As someone who reads resumes, applications, cover letters, emails, and listens to phone messages daily from potential associates, your words, your tone, your accuracy, and correctness are the absolute very first things I notice. A misspelled word, punctuation error, poor grammar (both written and spoken), and a negative tone will send you immediately into the No pile.

The second thing I always like to emphasize is mode of communication. By this I mean, follow my lead. If I reach out to you via the phone, please call me back. If I email you, please email me back. Do not change the mode of communication on me. This seems so simple—like whose turn it is at a four-way stop—but you would be surprised how many times I give up on candidates because they don't follow this simple rule of communication etiquette.

Always remember that as you begin to take that next step toward your "High Gear Future," communication is key. Daily you will be asked to communicate in some form. Do it well, put thought into it, and use it as a tool to set yourself apart from the others.

To reach your dreams, you have to be able to see them. To live them, you will have to be able to communicate.

We agree with Patti! One tip I also share with students is this: Communication is not just about emails. You cannot be high gear if you are not out meeting and talking to people. In our firm, often one of my associates will send an email to a client and think that is the end of her task. Clients are busy, and they aren't at their computers or watching their smartphones for your email. It is important to consider when communication via email is better or a phone call. Furthermore, if you have confusing or complex issues, a phone call to ensure understanding by both parties is essential. A lot of meaning is lost or misunderstood when we text and email. I think successful business people use talking more and in-person conversations to really get things done.

ANNE

Emotional intelligence—the ability to manage one's emotions and perceive others' emotional needs and triggers—and soft skills can be the tipping points in an employer's decision to hire one person over another. Hone these skills in college so you can immediately add value to the workplace.

The National Association of Colleges and Employers released its 2015 survey on "Skills/Qualities Employers Want in New College Graduate Hires," (www.naceweb.org). The top five attributes are leadership, ability to work on a team, communication skills (writing), problem-solving skills, and strong work ethic.

Write your resume and professional story using these skills as your keywords. Notice that these are soft skills that can be learned and practiced daily. My middle son, Aaron, graduated from Penn State University with a degree in Wood Products Marketing. At his commencement, there were less than 10 graduates receiving diplomas in that major—at one of the biggest institutions in the country. Although he graduated in 2010, smack in the middle of the Great Recession, he landed a job immediately after graduation.

Take every advantage of career fairs at your school and introduce yourself to recruiters. Start conversations and ask questions. Aaron met the owner of a lumber company at a PSU career fair on campus. He was a PSU grad, and when Aaron introduced himself, they discovered that they had many common interests like hunting, the outdoors, forestry, and football. There was a likability factor recognized by both and a comfortable chemistry. Before the owner ever received Aaron's resume, he had formed opinions about Aaron from those first impressions.

What really matters in first impressions? Employers are looking for good eye contact, a firm handshake, a confident and relaxed body posture, appropriate dress, and an ability to communicate well.

That was five years ago. Aaron just accepted a new position in an entirely different industry this year. His interview process this time was extensive because the company was not a small business; it is an international, publicly traded construction materials firm. He submitted his resume online, not at a career fair. He then had an email followup, several phone interviews, an in-person interview, and a lunch interview with executives. Each touchpoint in the process requires a significant investment of time and money by the employer. The interview and talent acquisition process is lengthy, because it's very costly to hire wrong. And a wrong hire can become a protracted court battle.

After each personal interview, Aaron sent handwritten thank-you notes expressing his appreciation to the interviewer for his time and interest in him. This sends a powerful message of follow-through, attention to detail, and old-fashioned manners (which never go out of style!). The company decided to fill the position internally, but they told Aaron they liked him so much they wanted to create a new position for him. They felt he would be a great addition to their team.

After several months, they contacted him again with a fresh offer of a new position. The same interview process ensued, and when they made the final offer, he enthusiastically accepted. He again sent a handwritten thank-you note to his interviewers and sent it by FedEx, even though he lives only 20 minutes from the headquarters. Nothing says, "You're important" better than an overnight delivery of a personal thank-you note.

As we shared earlier, the first professional narrative your employer will see is page 1 of a Google Search of your name. Make sure you have Google Alerts set up for your name and for any misspellings of your name. This will help you protect your reputation.

In addition to your paper resume and story in Google Search, there is a tremendous opportunity to showcase your skills and experiences in your Twitter bio. Monica Bishop is a 2015 PSU grad. Her Twitter bio includes @penn_state Alum, Public Relations,

Communications, Event Coordinating, Founder of @TSouthernWave, Harrisburg, PA, and Nashville, TN.

These are all examples of activities, interests, and organizations. A PR agency can quickly glance at this and see that she's serious about her career and understands strategic social media use. A glance at her Twitterstream reveals that she tweets interesting content, articles about women and business; and she regularly participates in Twitter chats. All things a potential employer will be very impressed with. And most importantly, this is content that will appear on page 1 of Google Search.

My youngest son, Benjamin, graduated from Belmont University in Nashville, Tennessee, in May 2014 with a degree in Entertainment Industry Studies. Thanks to his college education, he understands the "business of music" and how important social media is to connect with record labels, fans, booking agents, tour managers, business managers, sound engineers, and venues. He signed a record deal with Sony Music Nashville in October of 2014. What was the first resume Sony discovered when they did a Google Search? Songwriter, Guitarist, @BelmontUniv alum, PSU, Eagle Scout BSA, Hunter, Fishermen, Avid Outdoorsman.

Last year he was invited to perform for the Boy Scouts of America National Annual Meeting which was held in Nashville. The National Eagle Scout Association Director had emailed him to invite him to perform for the Scout leaders. It was a wonderful experience and afterward Ben asked him how he found his name.

"I Googled 'Nashville Eagle Scout Country Singer' and 174,000 results came up. Your name was in seven of the top eight results. I checked out your website and Twitterstream, and that's how I found you." That's the power of your digital tattoo acting as your resume.

The new resume? It's 140 characters.

Masai Lawson, Manager of Talent Acquisition for Gannett Fleming, Inc.—a 2,100-strong global infrastructure firm that celebrated its 100th anniversary in 2015—sees hundreds of resumes each month and meets hundreds of potential job candidates. To make it easy for job seekers to learn about Gannett Fleming, the culture, and the caliber of work they do, she made a short video for YouTube titled #JoinOurJourney. Masai knows that candidates will research a company, check out the social media profiles, the website, and then ask, "Do I see myself working here? Would I fit in? I wonder what the company culture is like?"

Masai hopes engineering candidates do see themselves fitting in at Gannett Fleming, and she shared some tips from across the interview desk on how students can prepare to submit resumes.

Tips on Creating a Great Resume

1. When listing internships on the resume, instead of providing your list of duties, highlight active participation in meaningful projects and the contribution you made.

2. The Objective that most candidates list on the top of the resume does nothing to really sell who you are. Keep in mind a resume is a marketing tool, designed to grab the attention of a hiring manager. The ultimate objective is to find a job! Use that valuable space at the top of your resume to sell your brand, who you are, and why a company should consider you above the other 100 applicants that submitted resumes.

3. The resume should be easy to read. Use a bullet format to highlight Experience and Accomplishments versus narratives. Also make sure grammar and spelling are on point. A company is not going to hire an English major with poor written communication skills.

4. Don't rely solely on the resume. Reach out to people in the companies that interest you and make connections. Let them connect a face with a name. It may not pay off immediately, but you should always put some energy into expanding your professional network.

One strong word of caution on creating your resume: be honest! According to www.GradSchoolHub.com, 78% of resumes contain misleading information. Exaggerated job titles or responsibilities are in the top seven resume lies. Padding, stretching the truth, embellishing facts—it's all dishonest. Don't take part in these practices. Careerbuilder said that 58% of hiring managers have caught a lie on a candidate's resume. "Trust is very important in professional relationships, and by lying on your resume, you breach that trust from the very outset," said Rosemary Haefner, vice president of human resources at CareerBuilder.

What do employers consider a lie? A bright young college graduate asked me if I would be a professional reference on his resume. I had limited first-hand experience of his job skills and it only pertained to a few projects, but I agreed.

When another individual showed me his resume, and I read some of his accomplishments, I knew there was serious embellishment and at least one lie. The resume read, "Acquired corporate sponsor and coordinated radio/television coverage." How did I know that it was a lie? Because I was the one who acquired the corporate sponsorship. When he was confronted with the exaggeration, he unbelievably justified it by contending that we couldn't have achieved a corporate sponsor without his skills that led to the kind of success that would attract a corporate sponsor. It didn't matter to him that he never spoke with the corporate sponsor, never communicated with them about the sponsorship, and never was involved with the negotiations or deliverables.

He included it on his resume to make him look more accomplished and influential than he was. It was egregious and more revealing about his capacity to believe his own lies and to be comfortable with blatant dishonesty. Don't resort to fiction and dishonesty on your resume. And if someone asks you to be a reference on their resume, make sure you see the document first to confirm its truth.

CHAPTER 5

DNA, Drive, and Your Potential

"I have not failed. I've just found 10,000
ways that won't work."

THOMAS A. EDISON

We have talked about your digital footprint, and why that is so important. Equally important—and maybe even more important—is how you are wired, and what is in your DNA. DNA is something we cannot change, but knowing more about yourself and studying your family history can be powerful. Ask your parents and extended family members about their aptitudes and talents. Are your parents in leadership positions? Do they have strengths in math? Science? Communications? Your genetic blueprint—how you are wired—can be helpful in understanding your own strengths and blazing your own path to success.

Our collective 35-plus years as business owners has taught us many lessons beyond the classroom. Experience is the best teacher. **Focus on what you can do, not what you cannot do.** You cannot control other people, but you can control your reaction to them, and you can choose what to focus on. Know what your strengths are, and use them to your advantage.

Drive—your ability to self-motivate and cling to your aspirations in the face of all odds—comes naturally to some, and others have to conscientiously work at it. Whether you're born with grit or have to daily practice perseverance, your drive is directly related to your earning potential. Indeed, "Nothing can stop the man with the right mental attitude from achieving his goal; nothing on earth can help the man with the wrong mental attitude," said Thomas Jefferson.

AMY

Can people learn to be driven? I don't know the scientific or biological answer to this, but I can tell you from experience that I believe it can be learned. And don't confuse drive with personality and extroverted behavior. I know plenty of extraverts that are not driven. And I know some introverts who are. So how do you become or learn to be more driven? By watching those who are and then actually doing what they do. I think you must practice being driven. And I think there are two fundamental characteristics related to driven people: self-discipline and the ability to prioritize and see what is most important.

We talk about this in our first book, but an example would be—for a student—the choice to sleep in late or get up, exercise, and get ahead of homework assignments by doing work in advance. Sure you need to sleep late now and then, but there is truth in the old saying "the early bird gets the worm." I am a big believer in doing things in advance and completing tasks before they are due. Sometimes procrastination works, but in my 25-plus years in my career, I will tell you that more positives have come out of being ahead of the curve.

An example of being driven early in my career was a resume writing class my friend and colleague Elise Mitchell (CEO, Mitchell Communications Group) and I produced and taught to college students. We were both newbies in PR in Memphis when we came up with this idea. It generated additional revenue for us and allowed us to meet some great candidates. Elise and I also recall fondly when we got our first car phones. Back in the day, they were literally installed in your car so that you could talk while driving. I couldn't wait to get mine (they were very expensive to install and to use back then) and Elise was the first person to call me on my car phone. We probably could not afford them but knew if we were to be taken seriously in the business world, we had to invest in ourselves. I am proud to say Elise is a highly successful business woman who launched and grew one of the top communication firms in the country. She spends her time flying around accepting awards, speaking, teaching, inspiring and working. High gear starts early!

Early in my career I was in a meeting and a vice president of a company we were working with invited me on a tour of a new facility followed by a lunch with some key power players. I was able to go because I had finished—in advance—a major proposal we were working on for the U.S. government. It was a lengthy form that required more than 20 hours of work, but I had finished it early that morning before anyone else was at the office. My boss was impressed, and also surprised I think, and I was able to go on that tour because I had already completed my job for that day. This opportunity was an amazing career-builder for me.

How driven people achieve high gear:
1. Driven people work really hard at any goal. For a college student being driven means you put in the extra work to ensure you have done everything possible for that good grade.
2. Driven people don't get distracted, and they keep their eye on the goal. An example of this would be not skipping a class for a social diversion.
3. Driven people look for better ways to solve problems and collaborate. I tell my clients that "more heads are better than one" when it comes to ideas, creativity, and problem solving.
4. Driven people are frustrated by those who are not. I have almost zero tolerance for people who cannot get things done. It is both a blessing and a curse. Again, you cannot control what others do, but you can control how you interact with them.

5. Driven people don't accept No easily. Recently a CEO of a large company here in Memphis told someone "When Amy is told No she hears Yes." Not always. But the point is that driven people navigate obstacles and keep looking for the Yeses.

6. Driven people are usually successful at most things they attempt because they have both the right aptitude and attitude. Negativity and problems will come along, but how do we respond? Failure and challenges abound. Learn your lessons and move forward.

Can you add to this list? What drives you to your goal? Write these down in the margins of this page and come back later to revisit them. What are some other characteristics you see in driven people? Who are the driven people in your life? Find them and communicate often with them.

Zoe Raetzman, Senior, Texas Christian University

In the wise words of Colin Powell, "There are no secrets to success. It is the result of preparation, hard work, and learning from failure." At first glance this quote may appear as common sense, but there is beauty in the simplicity of this statement. Today, the media has an enormous effect on how individuals define success. Our perceptions of ourselves are no longer based on our own merits, but rather in comparison to what numerous celebrities and gossip magazines tell us. Much of my generation will go to great lengths in order to avoid working hard; we lack patience and expect instant gratification. While many desperately wish for a secret to success, there are some of us who still believe in the power of hard work.

No matter what your personal definition of success is, it should have nothing to do with other people. Many people fail to grasp that, and instead cause their success to be dependent upon the accomplishments of other people. Success is purely a measure of your own achievements and goals. And the only way to truly be successful is to utilize your natural abilities and work really hard to develop them. If you do, you will create a substantial competitive advantage that will set you apart and set you free.

Serena Silvan, Senior, Texas Christian University

DNA is essential in today's job market as connections, referrals, and mutual friends help you become more successful in landing your dream job. As for me, my family has connected me with many highly known individuals that have helped me obtain numerous internships, as well as a full-time position. My advice to any student would be to use your parents and their connections to the highest of your ability as they have already created and established their foundation to create a successful future. Their generation is already familiar with the working community, and they may also have many connections that they have already created throughout the years that you can use to your advantage.

Drive is what pushes you even further to becoming the strong, independent individual that you have always strived to be. You need to be that student in high gear that attends professors' office hours, never misses class, is attentive, listens, and more importantly, is always wanting to learn more. You have that dream, that passion, and that drive to accomplish great things. Know what you want, have a vision, and chase after it. If something gets in the way or if you fail, use it as a learning lesson and an experience that will only make you stronger.

ANNE

As Amy said, "Driven people don't accept No." You will hear the word No thousands of times on your way to high gear, but don't let it jolt you off course. To reach high gear, you have to put on your emotional resilience armor and be prepared to overcome the Nos. There will be many of them on the road ahead. Learning to withstand the Nos now in your 20s will be vital preparation for developing as a leader in your 30s and 40s.

In the May 2015 issue of *The Wall Street Journal Magazine*, the editor, Kristina O'Neill, writes: "Achieving success requires a number of factors—skill, luck, and patience among them. But perhaps the most important quality . . . is drive: the ability to single-mindedly pursue a goal even when it seems the whole world is against you."

In the past few decades we have seen a measurable trend in what psychologists and counselors call helicopter parents. These are parents that hover over a child, monitoring every move, filling every day with structure, and making sure every need is met. These children won't have the opportunity to develop their own drive.

What's the reality for these children as they grow up and prepare to go to work or college? Lori Gottleib wrote a compelling article in *The Atlantic* that gives insight on the issue. She reached out to Jean Twenge, a co-author of *The Narcissism Epidemic* and professor of psychology at San Diego State University, and shares:

"People who feel like they're unusually special end up alienating those around them," Twenge says. "They don't know how to work on teams as well or deal with limits. They get into the workplace and expect to be stimulated all the time, because their worlds were so structured with activities. They don't like being told by a boss that their work might need improvement, and they feel insecure if they don't get a constant stream of praise. They grew up in a culture where everyone gets a trophy just for participating, which is ludicrous and makes no sense when you apply it to actual sports games or work performance. Who would watch

an NBA game with no winners or losers? Should everyone get
paid the same amount, or get promoted, when some people
have superior performance? They grew up in a bubble, so they
get out into the real world and they start to feel lost and helpless.
Kids who always have problems solved for them believe that they
don't know how to solve problems. And they're right—they don't."

In our quest to fill these pages with the best insight and wisdom
possible for students, we received some Nos. We asked some leaders
to participate, and they chose not to or were unable to. We didn't
decide to table the book idea just because some of our potential
contributors said No. We didn't close our businesses the minute a
client challenged our decisions. Maybe it's because we're both in
public relations, but we have developed thick skin with the word No.
What if we never revisited a reporter to pitch a great story because he
had turned us down once for an idea?

During the writing process for *Students in High Gear*, we had
interruptions and obstacles and businesses to run. John C. Maxwell,
author of *The Difference Maker*, writes: "You can tell the caliber
of the person by the amount of opposition it takes to discourage
him. Orison Swett Marden, founder of *Success* magazine, observed,
'Obstacles will look large or small according to whether you are large
or small.' Big people overcome big obstacles."

During college and post-graduation, embrace an attitude of
"Let's overcome and get it done." Early in my editorial career at a
publishing house, the executive editor gave me a writing assignment,
and it included getting a source quote from an individual. When I
submitted my article, I explained that I couldn't reach the individual
and therefore didn't get the quote. He handed the article back and
said, "Well, try again. Get the quote." It was a great lesson for me that
to reach your goal you have to be persistent—doggedly persistent.
He refused to accept No. And you shouldn't accept No for a final
answer either. Find a way to reach your goal.

Now as an employer, I look for people to hire who have that intangible quality called drive. People who are overcomers and are not afraid or easily discouraged to think big. They can see a goal and work independently at reaching it. If you hire people who are so emotionally fragile that you feel you cannot be honest with them or they'll collapse in tears, then you've hired the wrong person.

Driven people aren't perfect people, but they find ways to get the job done despite the odds. They are emotionally resilient when the Nos come. Develop that kind of drive and high gear is within reach.

CHAPTER 6

The Cumulative Effect of Choices

"Remember that guy that gave up?
Neither does anyone else."

UNKNOWN

Regardless of your age, one of the most powerful choices you will always have—at school, at work, and at play—is who to spend time with. If renowned author and businessman Jim Rohn was correct, "You're the average of the five people you spend most of your time with." Are your friends smart, ambitious, hard-working, well-read, on-time, have a good sense of humor, and able to laugh at themselves? That's a well-chosen group of friends. Look for friends outside of your interests so you can appreciate lots of viewpoints and learn to appreciate different perspectives. That doesn't mean you compromise your own views or values, but it does mean you'll begin to learn how people who think differently can work together.

The day-in, day-out choices you make are cumulative. **Making great choices daily leads to success in life.** Making good choices leads to opportunities that lead to successes. How do you make good, strategic choices?

AMY

How often have you heard someone say, "I really don't have a choice." Sometimes this is true, but it is only acceptable if you have truly exhausted every resource within your power. There is a lot to say about free will and choices. In high school, you don't have as many choices because as a minor, your choices are limited by the ones your parents allow for. At least that's the case in our home. I will say that my kids make good choices in general, but parents are there to steer the ship and teach you enough so that when students do go off to college, they are prepared.

I'm facing this transition with my son right now. As I write this he is 19 and is a college freshman. I knew I was going to cry when he left for college, and I dreaded that day. But this is also why we are writing this book. We want our own children to be high gear students in school and later in life. Anne's sons are grown now, living high gear lives working and starting families. Mine are in high gear high school and college mode. So writing this book is important to us as we are living in the midst of the craziness of it all.

Once at college you are like a bird out of a cage. No more parents checking your time for curfew. Nobody telling you where you need to be and reminding you to pick up your room. You are passing over that milestone of teen turning young adult.

I'd like to tell you how I went from a public high school to a prestigious liberal arts college in Memphis. I wish I could tell you that it was because I was valedictorian or something impressive like that. I got there for two reasons: first, because I could outwork others; and second, because I had a lot of support from graduates who knew me in Mobile and encouraged me to apply at Rhodes. They wrote letters for me, made phone calls, and even took me on a roadtrip to see the campus. I had already received a full scholarship from the University of Alabama (so Roll Tide Roll to you Alabama fans out there). Alabama offered me a "Leadership" scholarship—for four years—for my high gear high school leadership and awards. Instead, I chose to apply to Rhodes, was accepted, signed up for student loans to get there and helped my parents finance my college years at Rhodes. It helped me that Alabama had offered me that scholarship, and that was certainly leverage to apply to Rhodes. To the students who don't test well—I made a 19 or 20 on my ACT and that's it. Back in the day, we didn't have testing prep tools and tutors. We took the test and that was it. I don't even recall students taking it more than once actually.

I know test scores are a big deal today for students (because colleges rely on them), and unfortunately they are not—in my opinion—high gear markers. I believe the higher educational institutions that deny applicants due to an ACT score are missing the boat. Furthermore, these scores should not be so heavily weighted as we believe they can be a barrier to success. So if you don't test well, you must play to your strengths in other areas and not be discouraged. Let me be your example of someone who did poorly on standardized testing and had to work really hard to maintain Bs in tough subjects—sometimes Cs. And it turned out pretty well for me, so you can do it too! You just have to work harder and be more creative in your scholastic experience. And don't be discouraged if you don't get accepted to your first choice of college—embrace those that do accept you and fly with them. And I will give you a tip: Your teachers can be your most important high gear allies. Get to know them and ask them to help you if you are struggling.

When I got to Rhodes College (back then it was named Southwestern At Memphis) in 1982 in Memphis, I had never been away from home for any extended time, and I certainly was not familiar with a city like Memphis. Living in Texas and Alabama—Memphis was like a whole new world to me. My parents loaded up a pickup truck they borrowed and drove me to school. We unloaded my stuff which I had been purchasing for this new adventure—shower caddy, towels, bed linens. We didn't have computers and fancy electronics so we bought phones—real land lines that plugged into the phone line in our dorm rooms. And we only had one. I think my Mom cried all the way back to Alabama, but I was as happy as a jaybird. I made friends fast, loved the college social life, and loved my roommate and suitemates immediately.

I pledged Chi Omega and made great friends and sisters in that sorority. This was my first good choice as these are great women and still my friends to this day. We don't see each other often, but Facebook has certainly reconnected everyone.

I also made the right choice to switch my major to English from trying to pursue medicine. Dr. Mortimer, the chemistry professor, was my advisor and in short order told me science and math would not be my strong suits. I listened to his advice, switched to English, and spent four years playing to my natural strengths. I chose other classes based on my interests and passions and studied hard. I had to study hard to pass, and I knew that. Hard work in high school had paved the way for college, and I knew how to study, organize, and get work done on time. A very important skill for a student to grasp is the ability to prioritize. Do the important things first.

Another great thing I did—not by choice but by necessity—was work in the athletic department for those four years. My freshman year, as low woman on the totem pole, I had to work the concession stands often flipping burgers and cooking hotdogs for all the other students attending the games. So, think about that for a second: while all of my friends were attending games, I was behind a grill prepping and fetching their food. Kind of humiliating at the time, but a great life lesson, and something I think that made me appreciate my college opportunity. Later, as I progressed, I got to work in the office and as a lifeguard at the pool for several years. This work-study program at Rhodes helped me pay my way through college and learn the balance of getting school work done and working. (As a side note and benefit: While working in the athletic department I got to meet the then "Memphis Showboats" a USFL team that practiced at Rhodes. I met the great Reggie White prior to his playing for the NFL—it was a fun year when we had those "Memphis Showboats" in town.)

Now another choice and important decision I made in college was to *not* skip classes. This was a big deal at Rhodes then. I think some of our professors took roll and some did not. Rhodes operates on an honor system and as students we pledged to do our best and pledged to go to class. Some took that seriously, and some did not. I did. Plus, I had skin in the game. I was paying for my own education, so why waste it?

Going to every class was my commitment to myself and to my parents who were also sacrificing a lot to send me there. I viewed time in those classes as cash and helping pay for it—I think—gave me a sense of dedication. By helping out financially, I had skin in the game.

But the real reason I didn't skip class is because I'm not naturally a genius. I didn't test well in middle and high school; my grades were good—good enough to be in the National Honor Society in high school. But I had to work really hard at it. In college, I went to class because I knew it would give me a better advantage, and I had to if I wanted to pass. I studied *in class* by listening and taking notes and really focusing every brain cell on what was being taught. I think that is half the battle and many of my friends would spend hours cramming for tests and stay up all night to study. Again, good choices are cumulative. Studying in class (Tip: sit in the front row if you can so you don't get distracted) meant I already knew the material when it came to test time. I was one of those who could not stay up all night! Sleep is a brain enhancer, and I don't do as well without much sleep—a fact I also knew about myself. It is still true today.

The other choices I made in college were to get involved in leadership programs and contribute to programs and projects like fundraisers that made a difference in our community. When our annual funding campaign kicked off my senior year, Rhodes' Office of Development selected me to be the senior student representative to help with student fundraising. I said yes to that, not because I wanted it for my resume, but because it was a good thing to do, and I was passionate about giving back. Later, I was named class president (Class of 1986) where I continued to raise money and plan reunions for Rhodes for more than a decade after graduating. Today I have reconnected with Rhodes, and they are participating in this book. They are doing amazing work and producing students in high gear. It's important to me to stay connected to my alma mater. A high gear goal for me some day would be to teach this book at the college and continue to serve Rhodes in different capacities.

Here are my DOs for making choices in college:
1. Surround yourself with friends who share your same objectives and values.
2. Get enough rest.
3. Exercise and eat healthy whenever possible.
4. Go to class, get to know your professors, and ask them to mentor you.
5. Start looking for resume-building activities you have a passion for.
6. Pay attention to the city you are in and read the news.
7. Listen to your parents and leverage the power of their connections.
8. Start building your social media platforms in positive ways.
9. Seek mentors and internships in the business world.
10. Start your career search early and apply for as many jobs as you can.

ANNE

We can't overemphasize the need to make good choices throughout high school and college. You truly control your destiny (and it's important to realize that your parents don't control your destiny), and in America, the opportunities to find your passion and be a difference maker are limitless. College admissions officers and employers are looking for well-rounded individuals. They're not expecting GPAs of 101.5% from students who are in several extracurricular activities. Look for opportunities to show leadership in high school and use that as a training ground to lead initiatives in college and beyond.

I had a recent conversation with a high school junior who was asking a teacher to write a reference for his college application. The teacher asked him to write some highlights of his activities and experiences so he could review them before he sent a final version of his recommendation. "What do you see as your contributions to senior high? What activities are you involved in? Why should a college accept you? What fresh perspectives would you bring to campus life?" All good questions. I was helping him walk through some of his answers.

"I didn't really do a lot of activities," he said. Throughout our conversation, I noticed that he had a natural tendency for debating. With a smile, he had a good answer for every idea I suggested to include. Finally, I said, "You should join the Debate Team. You're confident in disagreement and have ideas and opinions that you like to express." "We don't have a Debate Team," he said. "All the better! Start one!," I replied.

Choosing to accept a leadership role in any organization or club is a great way to learn the life skills of persuasion, collaboration, communication, and community service. And it's the No. 1 attribute that employers are looking for in college graduates.

Several students came to my husband a few years ago with the idea to start an Outdoor Club at school. They had done their research and gathered enough people to form an active club, but they needed a Teacher/Sponsor. The group approached Corey because they knew he is an avid outdoorsman. They asked if he would be the Sponsor. After reviewing their charter, he was honored to represent them and the group was formed. These high gear motivated students made the ask. That's a powerful achievement to list on a college or job application. Where you see a gap, make the choice to fill it.

It's a similar exercise for young people applying for a job. The best applicants can understand the mindset of the recruiter and tailor the application to the prospective company's needs. Consider: Why should the employer hire you? Why are you the best candidate? *Have your good choices positioned you to be the best choice for an employer?*

Choosing the right trade school or college and then the right major are critical in helping you reach high gear. One of my first college visits was to a large University. It was a rainy Wednesday and the dismal weather might have had a negative influence on my decision. I had chosen medical technology as my major, so we spent some time seeing the facilities and learning about that career path. I decided against that institution for several reasons and accepted admission into Shippensburg University, in Pennsylvania, that was much smaller, but had a well-respected medical technology program.

After three weeks in General Zoology as a freshman, I realized that I had made the wrong choice. I called my parents to inform them, but I had to navigate the drop/add change-your-major process myself and very quickly find a new major to declare. My parents didn't drive up to campus to walk me through the process or put me on speakerphone to walk me through it. They supported whatever choice I would make.

I chose Communications/Journalism/PR. In tenth grade I wrote a report on *Lord of the Flies*, and my English teacher gave me an A and wrote, "You have talent! Well done!" on my paper. I never forgot that she felt I had a gift for writing, but I had never before considered it as a career choice. When I looked at my options, I saw Communications/Journalism/PR and had an Aha moment. My teacher's encouragement was one of the tipping points in my career choice.

If you remain with an Undeclared major for a year or two, choose a wide variety of courses to help you decide where your natural abilities lie. When former U.S. Secretary of State Condoleezza Rice realized that she was not going to be a concert hall pianist, at least for a vocation, she had to choose a new major at Stanford University.

Ms. Rice was in her junior year of college, and her parents were concerned that she hadn't chosen a course of study yet. She reminded them that it was her life; they reminded her that it was their money.

And so I went back to college in desperate search of a major. I had to make a quick decision, and so in the fall quarter of my junior year, I tried English literature. Now, with all due respect to the members of the English literature faculty out there, I hated it.

... Now it is the winter quarter of my junior year, and I decide that state and local government—that sounds really practical. Well indeed, my little project was to interview the city water manager of Denver, the single most boring man I have met to this day. And I thought, "It's not that, either."

And now it is spring quarter of my junior year, and I'm getting those letters from the registrar. "You cannot register again until you declare a major." And fortunately, I wandered into a course in international politics taught by a Soviet specialist—a man named Josef Korbel who had a daughter named Madeleine Albright. And with that one class, I was hooked. I discovered that my passion was Russian—things Russian, things international, diplomacy.

Needless to say, this wasn't exactly what a young black girl from Birmingham was supposed to do, but it was like finding love. I couldn't explain it, but I knew it was right. And you know something? Several years later, when I was working for President George H.W. Bush and Mikhail Gorbachev was in town, President Bush asked me to take Gorbachev back out to Stanford, where he was going to California to see more of the country. I sat on the South Lawn at the White House—Gorbachev, his wife, the Secret Service and me—and I thought, "I'm really glad I changed my major." (www.smu.edu/News/2012/commencement-Condoleezza-Rice-speech).

Find some entrepreneurs as friends—these young people will help you stretch your goals, think outrageously big, take risks, and get back up from failure or ridicule. Do you have any friends that are wrestlers? As the mother of three sons who all wrestled, this sport, above any other, helps young men (and women) turn failure into success every six minutes on the mat. The resilience and resolve a wrestler develops is life-changing. If you know them, chances are you'll learn some of their tips on getting back up after failure.

Here I'd like to add some high gear advice from James D. Dymski, Director Oncology Access, Reimbursement, and Distribution with Boehringer Ingelheim. Jim is my brother-in-law and an extremely driven and business-savvy executive. He holds two graduate degrees, one from Penn State University, and an MBA from The Ohio State University. He has mentored many young people as they enter the deep-end of job seeking, and I tapped his expertise on what he considers high gear attributes in the mentoring process. His decades of experience in large corporations and with the interview process is a career advantage for young people and on-rampers.

Your decisions affect your earning potential.
James D. Dymski, Boehringer Ingleheim

High gear young people are informed and take ownership of their decisions. I have been in multiple mentoring situations where individuals seem to be conflicted by the position they find themselves in. How did I get here? The answer—and without exception—is that the source of the dilemma can be contributed to two or three uninformed or emotional decisions. If we are to be informed and accountable for our decisions, then we need to consider what and who influences our decision making. Is the individual grounded by core principles that they have developed on their own? Or are they making decisions based on how someone else feels on the topic? There is an important difference.

Decision making is critical in determining your future:

1. You need to know who and what is currently influencing you.

2. Who is in your inner circle consistently speaking into your life?

3. What are you reading?

4. Who are you listening to?

5. Are they assembled with diversity of experience and thought?

6. Are they of different age groups and occupations?

7. Do you respect the decisions they have made? Would you want your life to take the course that theirs has?

8. Is your inner circle intentionally formed?

No matter what your decision-making process is currently; take time to reflect and write down the answers to the above questions. What and who are currently influencing you? Are these the type of influences that will provide wise counsel? Importantly, ask yourself, Have they been to where I want to go? Be objective. People can't give you advice and direction from a reservoir that is empty. This is a step in maturity.

When you assemble your inner circle, avoid group think at all costs. I recommend you intentionally develop a small diverse group of individuals to make up your inner circle.

This group will hold you accountable for your continued growth and keep you grounded. Build and refine this group from not only people you currently know, but network to add diversity of thought and experience to your inner circle. If you are a football fan, building your inner circle is like draft day without limits. You can add or subtract from this group without the burden of a salary cap.

The first intentional decision that will allow you to shift into high gear is to assemble your inner circle. I have three to four inner circles I rely on which focus on the following subject areas: career, family, spiritual, and financial. Who you invite in your inner circle will determine your altitude.

Now that we have considered the forming of the inner circle, let's take a deeper look at the anatomy of decision making. Decision making can be segmented into macro and micro levels. On the macro level, what is guiding your decisions? What are your core values that are the guard rails in your life? On the micro level, how consistent are you in applying these core values into your decision-making process? It is critical to have your core values consistent if you have more than one inner circle, because you will be faced with multiple decisions across a broad spectrum of areas as you ascend.

Core values need to be constant. Employers, peers, spouses, and even children value consistency. Decisions have a compounding effect. As your responsibilities increase, your decisions impact not only your life but others.

Leaders are individuals who are able to take on more responsibility and reap greater salaries as they demonstrate credibility in their decision-making ability. Your earning potential is directly tied to your decision making.

With independence comes accountability. For years the youth in any generation in every culture and pursuing all occupations have been told two fundamental truths: The first is to make good decisions, and the second is be selective about who you spend time with. I choose to emphasize this because it has been my experience that this is more often the case. Young people are *told* things. In the spirit of foreshadowing, odds are that you will do the same to your children and others you mentor, but you will lead them somewhat differently based on your experiences.

Through this slight course correction, you will be creating a competitive advantage not only for yourself but for those you influence. Here is the secret that you will not learn by checking someone's status on Facebook, Twitter, or Tumblr. The majority of individuals are told at an early age what to do, but not the why behind the directive. Students in high gear need to know the why behind these fundamental truths. Understanding why will create a competitive advantage for you. Knowing why will impact your relationships, your career choices, and your life. It will ignite your passion to not only grasp the truth, but to pursue it with intentionality.

As a society and culture, we have evolved in so many wonderful ways. Our life expectancy has dramatically increased from the turn of the century. Our standard of living in the United States is the envy of the world. We are all aware of the economic growth this country has experienced moving from an agrarian society where we were accountable for providing food for ourselves to leveraging the power of machines in the Industrial Revolution to the power of the techno-information age.

Advances in medicine, be it the area of diagnostics, surgery, or pharmaceuticals, have lengthened and prolonged our lives beyond what the imagination could comprehend just 50 years ago. Now that we're immersed in the 21st century, it is critical not to forget from where we have evolved.

To emphasize and add color to this picture, I am going to select several milestones my father-in-law experienced. Two major components drove every decision he made—his perspective and his core values. These pivot points were his constant companion throughout his life. His story is consistent with those of the Greatest Generation, as coined by Tom Brokaw in his 1998 book of the same title. Also called the GI Generation, these are Americans who came of age during the Great Depression and fought in World War II.

Brokaw wrote, "It is, I believe, the greatest generation any society has ever produced." He argued that these men and women fought not for fame and recognition, but because it was the "right thing to do."

We need to stop and ask what the "right thing" is. That answer depends on your perspective, the influences in your life, your family context, and above all, your priorities. The importance of this point is everything needs to be placed in the proper perspective. It is from an individual's perspective that one gains insight into decision making.

My father-in-law was born in 1921 and spoke of an early life of using an outhouse (no modern indoor plumbing). His early teens were influenced by the Great Depression and his late teens by the growing threat in Europe. In 1943 he graduated from college. Upon graduation, he elected to enlist in the Army in order to support a cause he deeply believed in. On rare occasions, he would speak of the fear and anxiety of leaving both his immediate and extended families to go off to England to face the Nazi war machine in World War II. Think of that reality as a graduation present!

Upon returning stateside after tours in England and Africa, he continued to contribute as an active leader in the Boy Scouts, the Jaycees, the Lions Club, and his church. While he did recently pass away at the mature age of 90 (after being married to the same woman for 60 years), in his lifetime after such humble beginnings he rode the wave of innovation and technology to own a cell phone, receive a pacemaker, and observe the real-time military war tactics of Desert Storm.

This is a living picture of diversity. This type of perspective is not found in your college club, athletic team, or your Facebook feed. The game is changing; therefore, the tactics need to change as well. Begin to augment your digital expertise with additional perspective beyond your own experience. This is the type of individual I would select for my inner circle. My father-in-law had experience and perspective I did not have.

When we first starting investing in each other, he was 67 and I was 23. Here is the key for anyone seeking to gain wisdom and perspective, both of which will provide a competitive advantage:

- Identify people who have been around the block more times than you have.

- Seek out and identify people who are where you want to be and ask for their counsel and insight.

- Move beyond your peer group.

This type of perspective will be a force multiplier in your life. Your perspective will be broadened and your core values will be polished.

Where does a 20-something find this generational perspective? Look for it at the local community level by attending a multi-generational church or network at a chamber of commerce, professional association, Rotary Club, scout troop, or Lions Club.

Life experience matters. As a student prepared to make an impact in the workforce, you need to temper your expectation as you enter this dynamic and exciting reality. The measuring stick changes when you receive a paycheck in today's economy and live beyond the classroom. As the measure of success changes, seek additional input that prepares you for your future.

As you enter this next chapter of your life, I encourage you to refine your understanding of how things actually work. To become an effective decision maker in both the marketplace of ideas and commerce, the rules of the game call for a perspective that will not be found as a bullet point in any course syllabus.

If you spend time reflecting on the eight questions on page 83, you'll begin your career with a fresh perspective and a stronger foundation to develop your earning potential.

CHAPTER 7

The Importance of Debt Control and Understanding Financials

"Live like a student when you are a student. If you live like a doctor when you are a student, you will live like a student when you are a doctor."

DR. LISA WADE

Debt is a real issue for today's students and graduates. If you search this topic on Google, you can see it is a national debate, and one the media has covered extensively. If you are going onto graduate school with undergraduate debt, you may want to consider a transitional job before graduate school investment. Too much debt can limit your career. If you have too much debt, you cannot afford to invest in yourself or explore entrepreneurship. Control your debt, pay it back, and do everything in your power to secure scholarships and strategically select schools that are within your financial budget.

AMY

The cost of college has increased exponentially. It's unfortunate that the cost of a college education has become unattainable for so many in our country. If you cannot afford a four-year college, consider a two-year community college or a technical school.

As I write this book, my son Bryan is starting his freshman year at the University of Memphis. My husband and I are making the financial decision not to borrow money for Bryan's college education if we can help it. Between what we have saved and what we can pay, we hope to avoid taking out loans. Additionally, Bryan has a job and will likely have several jobs through college to pay for expenses.

The bottom line is that every person must decide what is right for them. Each family has unique financial situations, and there are many ways to pay for college.

Dr. Lisa Wade, a good friend, is a Professor at Southern College of Optometry (SCO) in Memphis, Tennessee, where she serves as the Director of the Hayes Center for Practice Excellence. After a successful 20-year career in higher education, she took an eight-year hiatus to hone her business skills as an entrepreneur and purchased a Harley-Davidson dealership in 2006. During that time, Dr. Wade guided the dealership to Platinum Bar and Shield status and recognition as a Top 6 Performing Dealership in the U.S. She was recognized as Entrepreneur of the Year by the *Memphis Business Journal*, and one of the Top 50 Business Women in Mississippi by the *Mississippi Business Journal*. In 2014, she returned to academia to teach business principles and management skills. Dr. Wade is also the recipient of SCO's Lifetime Achievement Award for service to the profession of Optometry and the institution.

The Truth about Student Debt
Lisa Rossmeyer Wade, OD, MPA

The fat envelope from Ivy League U shows up in your mailbox, and you and your parents are thrilled that all those AP courses, service hours, and SAT prep courses have paid off with acceptance at your dream school. If your mind doesn't immediately rush to how to pay the $45,000-a-year tuition at Ivy League U, your parents' certainly will.

As you dig through the contents of the envelope, you see another document titled Financial Aid Award Letter. It says that you have been awarded $40,000 a year in financial aid. "WOW," you think. "Since tuition is $45,000, I only have to come up with $5,000 a year. I can make most of that during summer vacation! No problem!" But closer inspection shows $3,000 of your award is a scholarship, $2,000 is a grant, $2,000 is Work Study, and $33,000 is Student Loans.

What does this mean to you and your family financially? Essentially that only $5,000 of your financial award is FREE money, $2,000 will have to be earned working during the academic year, and $33,000 of it will require you, and possibly a family member, to sign legal documents obligating you to repay this money with interest over a specified time.

The reality for most students receiving financial aid is that at least a portion of their financial aid package will be in the form of student loans. The bigger reality is that the amount of student loan debt you will be allowed to take on by a college or university has no relationship to the earning potential of the degree you will receive from Ivy League U or even State U. Nor does it consider that you might not be able to complete your degree due to personal or financial issues, yet you will still have the obligation to repay a potentially large debt—with interest!

High schools use a student's acceptance to prestigious (read: expensive) institutions as a recruiting tool to enroll future students, as well as an advertisement for the perceived quality of their educational program. Parents and students have been conditioned to believe that turning down acceptance to an elite (again, read: expensive) institution is akin to committing personal and career suicide. In reality, the opposite might be true. Assuming that level of debt to attend your dream college may in fact be the real career suicide.

Do not read the above paragraph as a condemnation of well-known, well-regarded colleges and universities. They didn't become respected institutions without offering an exceptional education, the opportunity to make potentially life-altering connections, and opening doors that might otherwise be closed.

However, unless you have the financial resources to attend any college at any cost without incurring debt, for the sake of your future financial and personal well-being, you must have a thorough understanding of the consequences—good and bad— of taking on student loan debt.

The very excited student we encountered at the beginning of this chapter could be in for a lifetime of financial hardship. A four-year education at Ivy League U will require this student to take on a minimum of $132,000 in debt, just to cover the price of tuition, and I haven't even mentioned the other costs to actually enroll and attend a college or university. Is it worth $132,000 in student loan debt to have the satisfaction of attending your 10-year high school reunion wearing an Ivy League U sweatshirt and bragging about your Ph.D. in English and position as an Assistant Professor? The fact is that the earning potential early in your academic career is probably $30,000–$40,000 and tops out at $60,000 as a full Professor after 10–15 years.

We could even ask if it is financially sound to borrow $15,000 to attend State U for a STEM career, which traditionally has higher short- and long-term earnings than a career in academia.

The bottom line is that before accepting admission to ANY institution, you must completely understand the following four things:

1. **What is the total price of attending?** Tuition is just the start. You have books, activity, technology and lab fees, clothes, health care, housing, food, transportation, and travel at school and to and from home. Want to pledge a Greek organization? You might want to go to a movie or football game and have a pizza once in a while, and you have always dreamed of at least one Spring Break in Cancun! The price to attend Ivy League U is not the $45,000 in tuition, but approaching $65,000 to $70,000 in total expenses. Do a complete budget to determine the actual price to attend.

2. What is the total cost of attending? If you don't expect to need or receive financial assistance, the cost is the same as the price. However, if you expect to qualify for a Financial Aid Award, your total cost could be much less than the total price. Determine exactly what financial resources you have or will receive to decrease the cost of attending—parental/family contribution(s), grants, stipends, and scholarships—in order to calculate your total cost of attendance. *Remember, student loans do not decrease the cost of attendance, they increase the cost because they must be repaid with interest.*

Here is a frightening statistic: In a recent study by the Brown Center on Education Policy at the Brookings Institute, only 52% of students enrolled in a sample of selective public universities were able to accurately state the actual cost to attend their first year of college within $5,000! Twenty-five percent overestimated their cost, 17% underestimated the cost, and 7% stated they did not know.

3. Be aware that all financial aid is NOT CREATED EQUAL. You must understand what types of financial assistance make up your award. If it's all scholarships and/or grants that don't have to be repaid, terrific, but you still need to ask what are the conditions to maintain these? Is it a certain GPA, or work, or service requirements? What happens if you fall short of these requirements during one semester? Can you get them back, or are you on your own financially? What if a course you need is not offered and requires you to attend another semester to graduate? If you change majors, you are now looking at five years instead of four to complete your degree. Can you afford to stay if you lose some or all of your scholarship/grant money?

Most often, financial aid awards include some amount of student loans: subsidized or unsubsidized? There is a significant cost difference. What is the interest rate? Is there a grace period after graduation? What are your options if you become ill or lose your job for a period of time during the repayment period? What is the TOTAL COST of repaying the loan?

Don't accept any financial aid package without a thorough understanding of all terms, conditions, and repayment requirements.

4. What is the cost/benefit of attending a given college or university for your anticipated degree? Whether your parents can afford the full price or you are depending on student loans, at some point you and your family must ultimately make a judgment about the TOTAL COST of attending a particular college or university against the realistic earnings potential of the particular degree program you plan to pursue. Sounds mercenary, and in the ideal world one might pursue an education for education's sake, but in the real world, most people are attending college to prepare for a career and financial independence. Comparing the cost of your degree against your potential earnings is what economists call a cost/benefit analysis.

Once you know the total cost to attend a college or university, do the math. You must determine the relative worth of attending a particular institution for your anticipated degree, especially if you have to take on debt.

The importance of point 4 cannot be overstated. Let's assume you are the STEM student mentioned previously who has borrowed $15,000 to attend State U. What might your financial situation be immediately following graduation? Since you were a good student who received scholarships and lived frugally, you only had to borrow $15,000 in subsidized Stafford Student Loans at 4.66% to get your degree in Mechanical Engineering at State U. Taking the standard 10-year repayment plan, your monthly Student Loan payment will be approximately $157.

To easily meet this loan payment, you should have at least $1,570 in take-home pay every month in order to have a debt-to-income ratio of no more than 10%. A financial analyst would call this a manageable level of debt. "No problem," you say, since you have a degree in Mechanical Engineering, and you're probably right.

But wait, you just bought a new car in order to get to work, so your car payment is $340 month. Now your total monthly debt payments are $497. To maintain a 10% or less debt-to-income ratio, you now need to take home $4,970 per month.

"Hmmm . . . my total salary is $60,000, but if I'm careful with my money, I can cover this without too much trouble." With a $60,000 salary, your take-home pay, depending on where you live, will be approximately $3,665 a month after taxes and with no contribution to your 401k. Well, now your debt-to-income ratio is 13.5%. Financial analysts consider a debt-to-income ratio of 11%–18% as a challenging debt level. With careful budgeting, you can cover your student loans and pay the car note without feeling too much of a pinch.

This has you thinking, "Mom says I need to buy a condo at a low price and interest rate so I don't waste my money on rent. I'm thinking of making an offer on a condo near work that's a steal at $85,000." You are a smart cookie. It is a great time to buy real estate with interest rates at historic lows, and since you managed your finances well, paid all your bills on time, have no credit card debt, maintain a credit score above 750 which qualifies you for a 3.75% 30-year mortgage, and Mom and Dad will give you the $17,000 (20%) down payment you need as a graduation gift, you'd have to be crazy not to go ahead and jump on the condo, right? WRONG!

That relatively small mortgage of $65,000 (remember you put 20% down) is going to cost you $301 a month, not including the insurance required by the lender. This brings your total monthly debt payments to approximately $789. Your debt-to-income ratio has now jumped to 21%. This is considered a complex level of debt by financial analysts and carries considerable financial risk.

Let's quickly review. Our hypothetical student has BELOW average student debt ($15,000 vs. the National Average of $29,000) with an ABOVE average income for a new graduate ($60,000 vs. the National Average of $44,000). Even with a modest lifestyle, this person is potentially headed for financial difficulties, and at the least, faces the challenge of saving for retirement or emergencies. Imagine the financial difficulties this student could be facing with even $50,000 in student loan debt, much less $100,000 to $200,000.

Again, do not read the previous paragraphs as a screed against accepting student loans to obtain a college degree: nothing could be further from the truth. I took advantage of student loans to complete my professional degree, and it was the best investment I ever made.

Most financial experts strongly advise against taking on debt for a depreciating asset—one that begins to DECREASE in value as soon as it is purchased—a car, clothing, a vacation. On the other hand, borrowing money for an APPRECIATING asset—one that will INCREASE in value over time—such as real estate or a business can be a great investment if made with a thorough understanding of the risks and benefits of the type of loan and the full cost of repayment of the debt.

Is education an appreciating asset? The answer will often be a resounding YES! Study after study shows that individuals with college degrees earn an average of $1 million more over their lifetime than those without a degree; and this is just in salary. There are also added benefits such as health insurance, retirement contributions, disability insurance, life insurance, paid vacation, and sick leave that come with the types of jobs usually held by college graduates versus minimum wage or low wage positions.

Here is a very specific example. One individual takes out a $24,000 loan to purchase a new car. In 10 years, he has an asset valued at perhaps $3,000 to $4,000. Another takes a $24,000 student loan to earn a bachelor's degree in Finance, and in 10 years he is the Assistant VP at a major regional bank making $80,000 a year. Who made the better investment?

However, as with any other investment, borrowing for your education must be made with a complete understanding of risks and benefits. Here are some suggestions to help you make a reasoned decision about paying for your education:

Become financially literate. Not only is this the key to making good student loan decisions, it is vital to effectively managing all your financial affairs, including credit cards during college and beyond. Unfortunately, too many students and parents do not receive a good financial education. Websites such as CashCourse.org, debt.org, or greatlakes.org can be tremendous resources to improve your financial literacy and increase your understanding of the types of student loans, the mechanics and cost of repayment, the pitfalls of over-borrowing, how your debt-to-income ratio after graduation will impact your lifestyle, and more. If there is one piece of advice I can highlight, never sign any loan document without completely understanding your repayment commitment. Don't make a mistake that could cost you for years after graduation.

Understand that all debt is not created equal. Just like all financial aid is not created equal, neither are different forms of debt. As a college sophomore, $5,000 in student loan debt could mean you are in great financial shape, while $5,000 in credit card debt could indicate you are headed toward personal bankruptcy. One type of debt is an investment that can pay for itself hundreds, even thousands of times over during your lifetime. The other debt is a financial burden, that, if left unchecked, can stop you from having the ability to move out of your parent's house, get a job, or own a car—basically freezing you in adolescence and dependence on the kindness of others— even leading you toward personal bankruptcy. While all college students need and should have a credit card for emergencies and to help establish a good credit history, it needs to be a low-limit, no- or low-fee, low-interest card. My suggestion is that $1,000 should be the maximum limit any student has access to until he/she demonstrates a two- to three-year history of responsibly managing this financial tool. My opinion is if you are a student and have $3,000 or more in credit card debt that you cannot pay off immediately, you need credit or debt counseling now. The National Foundation for Credit Counseling can be a great place to start (www.nfcc.org).

Live like a student while you are a student. I tell my professional school students all the time: If you live like a doctor when you are a student, you will live like a student when you are a doctor. Incur the minimum amount of debt possible—student life doesn't last forever. Share expenses with a roommate. Ride the bus, carpool, or buy a used car. In five years, you can buy that nice, used SUV you've always wanted.

Make a monthly budget and stick to it. Nothing will derail your spending faster than not knowing where your money goes each month. At the beginning of every month, determine your budget for every expense and put cash in envelopes marked for rent, groceries, entertainment, gas, and more. That's what you spend—no more! If you have some left over, put it in your savings account. Next year, maybe you can borrow a little less money for school. Put the credit card in a glass of water and freeze it—it's for emergencies, not day-to-day expenses. Thaw it out when you have an emergency—not to order pizza. Don't go to Cancun for Spring Break. In five years, when all your friends are crying about their crushing student debt and how they are never going to be able to afford to go on vacation again, you'll be off to the sunny beaches with many fewer worries about your finances.

Ogden Nash, the American humorist, said, "Some debts are fun when you are acquiring them, but none are fun when you set about retiring them." I couldn't have said it better.

Borrow wisely.

ANNE

I'm the graduate of a state university in Pennsylvania. I am the third of four children in my family and our parents contributed (read: sacrificed) for our education, but we each had to work while attending college, and we each took out and repaid our own student loans. This is what we in business refer to as "skin in the game." My three sons did the same and all were expected to graduate in four years.

If it's your name on the college loan papers, then you are more likely to understand the monetary value of attending class, doing assignments, asking questions, and sticking to a four-year plan to graduate. A new phenomenon has occurred in the past decade and that's the propensity for students to take five years to graduate, or longer. Do you know who benefits from this? The college loan lenders because of interest payments, and the colleges and universities because they are providing the same required credits in five years as you would have received in four—you aren't receiving a more robust education, it's just taking you longer to acquire the credits to graduate.

Who is hurt most by this path? You and our economy. The U.S. will endure a weakened economic competitiveness with fewer skilled job seekers and fewer college graduates. And you, the student, will have one more year of tuition, room and board, food, books, and gas to pay for. It's an expensive trade-off for deciding to take 12 credits per semester versus 15 or 18. "Time is the enemy of college completion. The longer it takes, the more life gets in the way of success," (www.completecollege.org).

According to the National Center for Education Statistics, for students entering a four-year institution in 2006, only 39% graduated in four years. Females, in that same cohort, graduated at 43% while males graduated at 34.2% (www.nces.ed.gov). Consider what that lost year or two to stay in college costs; and more importantly, how does it affect your earning potential and the compounding interest effect of savings. *The Wall Street Journal* reported in August 2015 that nearly seven million Americans have gone at least one year without making a payment on their federal students loans. That's outrageous. That means 17% of all federal student loan borrowers are severely delinquent.

There are situations where your strengths and career goals will be a good fit with a private college—and that means an eye-popping tuition figure. If your private institution is out of state and costs $40,000 per year, think hard about your career path and your earning potential with a degree from that college. Remember to do a risk-benefit analysis.

Once you run the numbers, you'll have to decide if your earning potential and influencer network will outweigh the costs of the education. There are occasions where student debt is a good calculated risk and one that a student with high gear goals should take.

I'll share an example from our family. My two older sons graduated from Penn State University with degrees they used immediately after college graduation in their first jobs. They both graduated in four years. My youngest son, who always wanted to be a country artist, applied as a high school senior to Belmont University in Nashville, Tennessee. The tuition was $40,000 a year. Astronomical to us. In comparison, our first home cost $52,000. But knowing his guitar skills, career goals, his track record of self-discipline in reaching his goals, and his work ethic, it was a decision we supported. We did a risk-benefit analysis and felt he was worth the investment and his earning potential validated that decision.

We would certainly be sacrificing to help him attend Belmont and the drive was 12 hours from Pennsylvania. Ben was not accepted (great lesson in emotional resilience and determination) when he initially applied. He then applied to one of Penn State's branch campuses, Mont Alto. This was less than half the price of Belmont, and a one-hour drive from our home. Penn State also has the largest alumni association in the world. In any job interview, chances are high that a Penn State alum is an employee. Penn Staters form an immediate connection with each other, and that's a tremendous asset in a job search, a mentoring opportunity, or in an entry position.

Mont Alto was affordable and accessible, but not his original plan. He met with his advisor in the first week of classes and explained that Penn State was a segue for him to get to Belmont. Ben hadn't given up on his dream.

The advisor and the Mont Alto professors supported Ben's efforts to get the most out of his Penn State experience and make it count toward a transfer to Belmont in his sophomore year. He wanted to choose courses that would transfer because he knew that changing majors or institutions often results in adding an extra year to schooling.

He took 18 credits both semesters as a freshman, and he made Dean's List both times. He took advantage of the small class sizes and made sure every professor knew his name. He did the assignments, volunteered in class, and asked for help when he needed it. Stay visible in college; don't assume that big universities don't care about individual students. They certainly do.

When Ben re-applied to Belmont University in 2011, he was accepted. Why was Belmont so important, and why would we even consider sacrificing to help him get there? Dubbed the "Harvard of the music entertainment industry," Belmont University has a reputation for producing some of the world's best entertainers, singers, musicians, sound engineers, and record label executives in the world. The campus is located in Nashville, Tennessee, known as Music City. To shorten his learning curve and be living in the best city in the country for a musician, Ben needed to go to Belmont. It proved to be a pivotal decision in launching his music career.

He formed fast friendships with his professors who were musicians and some were still touring. Mastering the business of music is critical to achieving high gear as a musician. If you can't sell your songs and merchandise, then it's a hobby, not a job. And you can't pay the mortgage with a hobby.

"I can honestly say that I don't think I would have been signed by SONY Music Nashville—or any label—at the age of 22 if I hadn't gone to Belmont University," said Ben. "There are so many people who helped me connect the dots to reach my high gear; so many great songwriters who welcomed me in offbeat bars to listen and play some of my songs. I found most of my band members at Belmont and in Nashville. One of my best professors was Dwayne O'Brien, and we connected immediately. He is still my mentor today, and the first person I text when I have a touring question, or a band member question, or a music business question.

"When we opened for Little Texas, his band and one of my all-time favorite bands, it was the highlight of my tour! The guy who produced my first CD in a sound-proofed room in his apartment was a classmate from Belmont. He's on tour now as a sound engineer with Brad Paisley. The best advice I can give a prospective student is to grab everything college has to offer. Don't waste a minute. Take risks. Your future depends on it!"

CHAPTER 8

Curriculum and Careers Are Different

"The people who get on in this world are the people who get up and look for the circumstances they want, and if they can't find them, make them."

GEORGE BERNARD SHAW

Don't expect a college or university to teach you how to find your high gear or how to land your dream job. While they are certainly preparing you with every resource they have, it is up to each individual to take advantage of college resources. It is also important to realize that you can use your time in college to connect dots, build good relationships with professors, and network in and around your community. Today, it is a full-time job just to find a good job. You must leverage your passion and talents to blaze your own trail.

To maximize your college investment, you should think through the following questions:

- How does your major impact your career?
- How will you select courses that will fuel your passion for what you want to do later?
- Are you thinking strategically and selectively about your curriculum, and what classes will give you the best advantages in a competitive business environment?

Your choices of what you study can impact your future career. If you decide to major in engineering, for example, you have a multitude of career opportunities. If, however, you decide to major in art history, you must realize that most American businesses will never hire you to work on anything related to art history unless you are working for an art museum or auction house.

The key is to find your passion and figure out how to secure work in spite of selecting a niche area of study. Just because you major in something does not necessarily mean you will find a job in that area. STEM (science, technology, engineering, and math) is receiving a lot of press attention, and if you have strengths and passion in those areas it's a path to higher wages, career advancement, and personal fulfillment. In our first book, *Women in High Gear*, we explained that many C-suite professionals (CEO, CFO, COO, CIO) reached their executive positions from a STEM path such as finance.

For example, if you become a CFO (Chief Financial Officer) of a company, you likely majored in accounting and finance and worked in the financial services industry or for a CPA firm before being promoted. According to a 2011 *Forbes* article titled "The Path to Becoming a Fortune 500 CEO," 30% of Fortune 500 CEOs ascended to their positions with a strong background in finance. Developing financial acumen and understanding financial drivers for a business will be powerful high gear advantages for you. Usually someone in the C-suite has had a history of high gear career moves that include stints in finance and operations and has earned that position through hard work, smart choices, and dot-connecting.

Some students know right from the start what they want to do after college, but some do not. The good news is that now more than ever, colleges and universities offer so many choices and accompanying internship programs. High gear means taking advantage of the resources your school offers. Please, don't wait until you graduate. **It's never too early to start your career search!**

AMY

I majored in English at Rhodes College and graduated with my Bachelor of Arts degree in 1986. As I said earlier, I switched from Pre-Med to English due to necessity and the desire to graduate. Writing was both a talent and a passion. My Mom used to ask my Dad: "What in the world is she going to do with an English major?" For me, the answer was "Own and run a PR firm."

My major was the perfect choice because I could use my strengths, and I could communicate. Communication is critical in every business if you want to be a leader and ultimately move up the ladder in a meaningful career. Unless you are going into something deeply technical that requires working independently behind a computer or in a laboratory, communication is critical in business. I think it's everything.

It wasn't my major in English, however, that helped me secure my first job: it was my ability to persuade and communicate clearly. I had an aptitude for networking and the drive to meet people. I used my whole skill set to communicate why a firm should hire me right out of college. I didn't wait until after graduation to start my search.

During my senior year I read the local newspapers for job postings, worked with my advisors and placement office to complete my resume, and took advantage of every resource. I called businesses and asked advice on how to apply for jobs. I used my holiday breaks to interview and went on informational interviews where I would ask to interview the company. I would research and cold call to ask for a meeting to learn about their industry.

I studied magazines for what to wear to interviews and made sure I had a suit ready in my closet for any occasion. I was encouraged by the positive responses I received and how willing people were to help me. Make the ask! You never know how someone will respond until you do. Today unfortunately, it's a thousand times more competitive. That is why you need to be in a high gear career search.

I met some great Memphis business people through that process and started building my network. Eventually, I narrowed my opportunities between two: a job in a bank training program or a job at an architectural and engineering design firm. Upon graduation, I started my first real job as the administrative/marketing assistant to the CEO of Memphis's largest and oldest architectural and engineering design firm, Jones Mah Gaskill Rhodes, Inc.

While a lot of my friends were taking the summer off to travel in Europe or go on vacation, I was ahead of them working and nailing down my career start. And a prime reason was that my parents told me I would be off their payroll upon my graduation, so I was motivated to work. I was excited and happy to be employed by a firm that had growth plans and was in the process of designing all of the new hospitals for a large health care system in Memphis. The firm had a prestigious client list, and I knew I would meet fantastic people.

I had no idea what I had signed up for. Working for the CEO was a challenge, and my first project was to oversee the physical relocation of two large offices consolidated into one newly constructed, Class A office headquarters. Having never done anything like this, I called on my already established network of business people and hosted a lunch for a small group of influencers. I asked them about moving companies, if they had ever consolidated offices or experienced merging two large groups, how long it took to move, what type of labeling systems were out there for tagging furniture and equipment and more. Since I had no experience, I approached this as I would a research paper (remember, we had no Internet). I had to go find my resources and talking to experienced business people was the best first step.

The learning curve is steep and graduates who can shorten that curve are those who know how to communicate, ask questions, and listen. Good ideas are all around us; we just have to pay attention and listen to the pioneers who have forged a path. I didn't start my first job with my eyes on owning my own business someday. It took years of "connecting the dots" and working for other people to gain a lot of experience before I could strike out on my own.

High gear means you make good choices in each season of life. For me, this meant getting my newly consolidated architectural firm moved and in its new home properly, efficiently, and within budget. I knew that by excelling at this project, I would be given other projects that would propel my career. When you are in college, getting good grades and doing things that contribute to success (internships, fundraising, volunteering) are like compounding interest on money you have earned. Over time, achieving high gear pays dividends in your career and life journey.

In today's business world where technology is a differentiator, we have all kinds of options. Back in the late 80s, I had to physically be at the office to get work done. Today, we can work from wherever we are on a mobile device.

As an employer of recent college graduates and someone who hires interns yearly, I can tell you that not enough graduates interview at my firm with the right work ethic. Some I have interviewed in the past have asked me questions about how many hours they will have to work. I don't understand students who think they will become successful overnight or believe they can be successful by watching the clock. If you really want to succeed in business, you are going to have to devote both the time and the effort. Don't focus on vacation time and company benefits during your first interview.

College graduates need to know that a constant challenge for business owners is to attract and retain the right people. The hiring process is costly and time-intensive. I look for students who want to have skin in the game. I look for students who can communicate their passion and who understand my business model—either because they have studied it or because they have some experience.

As employers, we want team members who ask the right questions and understand the economics of a service-based business. Further, we want employees who are grateful for the opportunity to work hard, learn, and build a career.

I recommend committing to a job for at least three years. One reason is to demonstrate loyalty and your work ethic. In a professional services career, remember that your employer has a "Me x 3" rule. They will expect you to generate three times in revenue what you are earning to be a revenue driver to the company. For example, if you earn $40,000 annually, your firm will expect you to bill at least $120,000 in time. Following this advice will make you attractive to other firms and the kind of employee your current company wants to retain.

One of my recent college graduates who worked for us for three years found me on Twitter while still in college in another city. She studied our business and contacted me for an internship. I hired her as an intern, and then later, hired her full-time. She added great value to my firm through hard work and also promoting us and entering our work in various award competitions.

When she saw a national call for awards in Best Use of SEO (search engine optimization), she independently submitted Howell Marketing Strategies as a candidate. It was not in her job description to submit awards, but she thought it would be good marketing for the firm. When asked by her new employer if I would hire her again, my answer without hesitating was Yes. No matter where she goes, she will always have a great reference from me—her first boss.

As a graduate, if you can walk into an interview armed with information about my company, know about my competitors, ask questions about how we differ from other firms, and communicate your value, you have a chance at another interview and being hired.

Here are some first-person insights from Ken Cyree, Dean of The University of Mississippi's School of Business Administration (Ole Miss):

Ken Cyree, Dean of the School of Business Administration, The University of Mississippi

Being a college student is a great way to enhance success since students gain a lot of knowledge, but in general these students do not have much experience or the wisdom that is gained through experience. In my career, I have seen that most successful graduates are the ones who learn from others vicariously so that they do not have to make all of their own mistakes. To that end, it is important that college curricula and class content provide experiential learning. The learning can take place in the classroom with cases or applications, or perhaps from hearing outside professionals talk about their experiences. My preference is that the student intern or work in a chosen field to gain experience and make the classroom come alive with the richness of experiencing what the instructor is presenting.

Additionally, the experience that college students get while doing an internship is what sets them apart—or puts them in high gear. It is important to not only gain experience, but also to learn about the way things are done. In many cases, a student can find out that she does not like the field in practice as much as she did in theory. In other words, the field is not a fit for the student's skills or personality. Conversely, it can greatly enhance student passion if there is a fit, and can therefore solidify the chosen path and verify the decision is the correct one.

I frequently counsel students and parents on careers, and I often hear the two phrases, "You can be anything you want," or "Follow your heart and do what you want." I do not totally agree with either of these statements. For example, if a person passionately wants to be a professional football player, but is slow, small, and not especially strong, he would not have much chance at being successful in that profession. My advice is that this person focuses his passion into the business of football where he can get into high gear because he has a passion for the game. This might translate into working in the marketing department or helping the staff analyze draft picks. In general, the passion allows a person to maximize his potential in an overall area, but the correct fit is what allows that person to kick into high gear. Similarly, if a person has two options that are similar and one pays substantially more money, then it makes sense to me if the person chooses the one with the higher wages. I am not saying that a person should do something against her talents and passion, but rather she should consider whether or not she can make a living. It might seem romantic or noble to earn low wages by "following your heart," but it is also setting yourself up for real difficulties in life. Thus, to get to high gear, students should find what excites them and pursue it to the best of their abilities, while not ignoring the monetary benefits altogether. I do agree that for a person who pursues excellence, monetary success will follow, but I still recommend not ignoring the financial side of a career choice while following your passion.

Additional career advice that I give focuses on what to do in the job. In particular, I believe it is the proper goal to do whatever your job is to the best of your ability. I often hear things such as, "If I made more money, I would try harder," or perhaps "If they would incorporate my ideas, I would work hard." This is backwards thinking. Your responsibilities are a test and a stepping-stone to bigger and better things. Sometimes, college graduates believe they have all the answers and want to impress their new boss or colleagues with their knowledge, and then became disillusioned when their superiors do not embrace their ideas. I believe it is a good trait to ask questions and provide feedback, but at the end of the day it is the responsibility of your boss to make the decision about what to do. If you were the boss, would you want your employee constantly questioning what you are doing and then sulking when you do not follow his advice? Of course not. Treating others as you would want to be treated is the golden rule for a reason.

A high gear student learns to work hard at the task at hand and learn more about how to get better and grow in her career.

However, this is hard to do alone. I recommend finding a mentor to help you. Obtaining a mentor is not as hard as it sounds. In general, you ask others more experienced in a particular area questions about how to do things better. Most people are more than willing to help you if you ask, and this does not have to be a formal mentor relationship necessarily. Just having someone as a "sounding board" is often enough to help improve your performance and attitude.

Most people are flattered to be asked for their opinion, and if you are sincerely trying to learn, it is very unlikely they will refuse to answer your questions. However, don't ask a direct competitor to mentor you. For example, if you are competing with someone for bonus pay in a zero-sum game sales competition, they will have no incentive to help you since your success is their loss. Of course this is not the best way to maximize the efforts of the team, but some organizations still use this type of arrangement. The mentoring relationship might also be forced by having one assigned. If the relationship is assigned, it could be less effective from a relationship standpoint, but it might be very beneficial from a content standpoint since the person assigned to you could have skills that are more highly developed in a certain area where you need help. I believe regardless of the method, you should find someone who will help you learn, and therefore kick into high gear. And, it can be more than one person.

To me, the ability to maximize your abilities is a function of talent and ability coupled with motivation. We have already talked about choosing the right path to match your abilities with your passion, but one of the reasons that is important is because the passion allows you to work hard at perfecting your craft. In his book *Outliers*, Malcolm Gladwell stated that to become an expert it requires 10,000 hours of practice. I think it would be nearly impossible that someone could legitimately practice that much and dislike what they are doing. Recent research has shown little correlation between practice and becoming an expert and claims to have debunked Gladwell's theory. I think that the better explanation is that the people who practiced that much maximized their talent in that area, but clearly some are better-suited for certain activities than others. As a personal example, I have little musical ability, so no matter how much I practiced I could not be very good, but I would be the best I could be.

Another common theme for students who are successful is that they prepare well. Sure, talent in an area such as math or management can overcome a lack of preparation in some cases, but to be in high gear, preparation is key. Benjamin Franklin said, "By failing to prepare, you are preparing to fail." Thus, the professors and courses that require students to prepare well are helping them kick into high gear. If you couple passion and talent with preparation, that is the pinnacle for achievement for all of us, and award-winning professors help students reach the pinnacle by ensuring that students who are prepared are the most successful.

ANNE

Research reveals that college graduates who are job searching plan on staying in their first job two years or less. Starkly unlike the Boomers and the Greatest Generation, they are making job decisions based on short-term goals (www.experience.com/alumnus). The career path for Millennials now looks more like a zig-zag, entering and exiting whole and disparate industries with no desire to stay with a corporation for 20 or 30 years.

Young workers today will change jobs roughly eight times and careers three to four times. When you enter college, you should have some idea of your aptitudes—what are you naturally good at, what do you like to do, what do people recognize as your strengths, what are your passions? If you're unsure about your aptitudes and strengths, a great place to begin this discovery is to read *Strengthsfinder 2.0* by Tom Rath. This is a No. 1 *Wall Street Journal* bestseller and includes an online assessment tool.

Once you discover your strengths, you'll be clearer about a college curriculum choice. Don't choose a major based on your friend's major or your parents' majors. This is where a high gear career goal comes into play. Based on your strengths and aptitudes, what career choice is a good fit? And by good fit we mean a career where you can earn a sustainable family wage.

I am perplexed when I hear about college students that graduate in art history or exercise science but have not thought through what the career path is. Outside of becoming teachers, these students don't have a workplace view of available job opportunities in the art history field. How many art museum curator or gallery owner positions exist? There are limited jobs as museum curators or art auctioneers. High gear means you need to consider how you will make a living using the academic skills, experiences, and intellectual curiosity you've gained in college.

Another good place to research in-demand jobs is the U.S. Department of Labor Bureau of Labor Statistics and its projections for Occupations with the Most Job Growth. This report tracks job growth, projected growth, and salaries. If you have a passion for health care, accounting, software development, or home health services, you'll be in demand.

Sometimes your career revelations don't happen in the confines of a college classroom. Rachael Dymski is a good example of a young student who was uncertain of her career choice but decided that a trip out of the country might help her gain perspective and figure out a high gear career path. Rachael has a desire and heart for helping others. At Grove City College, in Pennsylvania, she loved her courses and professors, but felt no real passion or clear vision for any specific career. But when she lived in Costa Rica, she had a turning point.

The best thing I ever did to prepare myself for a career, or even to find my dream career, was to travel.

Colleges and universities encourage studying abroad and exploring jobs overseas for a reason. I think it's because when you're away from everything that is familiar; when you don't know the language, the culture, or how to get to the grocery store; when the buffers that kept you comfortable your whole life fall away, dropping in layers, you are left with only yourself. I don't know that traveling changes us as much as it shows us, for better or for worse, who we actually are.

The summer between my junior and senior year of college, I had very little idea of what I wanted to do after graduation. I had changed my major three times, and the program I was currently in didn't feel quite right. I received a scholarship from my school to spend a summer teaching in San Lucas, Guatemala, at an orphanage for girls.

Those three months I spent in the elbow of the tropics, where I watched the ground practically breathe out mangos and pineapples, where I walked to the local market for papayas and tortillas every Sunday, where I spent afternoons stretched out on a grassy soccer field trying to teach students math in Spanish, were some of the most defining days and moments of my life. During my time abroad, I was able to see amazing places, but I was also able to see, in a completely new light, myself.

To go to a place where the language and culture is not your own is to simplify yourself in a way that nothing else can. In Guatemala, with my halting Spanish, I was not worried about sounding eloquent or impressive; I simply worried about being understood. I was unable to hide behind catch-phrases or jokes. All of that fell away, until there was my stammering tongue, and behind that, only me. I had to relearn language, and along the way, learned that senses of humor, word pairings, and the rhythms of language are different everywhere. Latin Americans don't just say the word hot, caliente—they feel it with the rhythm and emphasis of their words. Speaking Spanish is like dancing—the language is a song.

Being away from my own daily routine made me realize just how much I depended on it to define who I was. I did not have my morning runs, because the area was not safe. I did not have hot cups of tea in the morning; I did not have a shower that worked. What I did learn, though, was that I had words. I loved writing in my journal; reflecting on my trip, trying to find new ways to describe the foods, the sounds, the scenery. I wanted to capture and express everything my broken Spanish could not. I found out, while abroad, that I had to write. It was what helped me put order to the world; it was what made me feel alive.

After all the layers, of comfort, convenience, familiarity were stripped back, I found myself. I knew what I wanted to do going forward, because I found something I was passionate about, away from the distractions of everyday life. I found a writer.

Samantha Bennett Gallaher, my daughter-in-law and a 2010 Penn State University graduate, agrees wholeheartedly with Rachael.

I am a first-generation college graduate, and although I sought the wise advice of my parents, much of my path had to be trial and error. I benefitted from strong adult influences in my life like my youth leader who is still a mentor to me. I began my college journey at a small Christian university in Pennsylvania. I had a church friend who had attended the college, but just before the start of classes, she decided not to return, so I found myself on a college campus with no familiar faces.

I was on the cross country team, so that provided an immediate network of friends for me. How could I have prepared better for my college experience? I had not planned on arriving with no friends. I should have explored the campus environment more and its surroundings. When I was in the dorm all by myself the first few days of cross country practice, I wish I had already discovered where the coffee shops, the stores, the bead shops, the grocery stores were. It was lonely those first few weeks.

My advice to college students: Go to any event they have on campus. Force yourself to step out of your box. It's the only way to grow and learn new things. I transferred to Penn State after my first year and met a whole new group of friends. One of the best experiences I had was choosing to study abroad. Through PSU's Human Development and Family Studies Program, we took classes in Italy for six weeks. We learned the same subjects but in a different culture. My experiences abroad continue to help me be a better teacher and employee. Stretch yourself and grow!

My internship is where I learned how to navigate the bridge between learning and doing. A fellow classmate recommended me for an internship, and from that experience I got my first job with an area YMCA.

With that in mind, here are my tips to maximize your college experience:

1. Make every effort to secure an internship and get hands-on experience in college. Seek extra learning experiences.

2. Ask more questions. Don't be afraid of anyone.

3. Be recognized for your positive efforts.

4. Make sure you interact with your boss, supervisor, and CEO. It took me three years to work on a project with the executive director. I asked myself, Why did I wait three years? I wish I would have asked her to work together sooner.

5. Work on emotional resilience. If someone criticizes your work, it's not a criticism of you as a person. You need to be able to accept constructive criticism to grow.

CHAPTER 9

Dot-Connecting and
Why You Must Master It

"You can make more friends in two months by becoming interested in other people than you can in two years by trying to get other people interested in you."

DALE CARNEGIE

There is a saying in business that your "network is your net worth." We love this because as seasoned business owners, we value building relationships over time and leveraging contacts we make along the way. We have benefitted greatly from years of putting ourselves out there to meet new people and make new contacts—especially in light of social media tools. This is more than just exchanging business cards, attending a chamber mixer, or conversing at a cocktail party. Real dot-connecting is a secret weapon and a strategic high gear activity.

We define dot-connecting as being able to identify influencers, understand what resources they provide, and then strategically forge a connection to create a competitive advantage for both parties. Dot-connecting requires knowledge of the big picture as well as details. It requires understanding what people do, why they do it, what drives them, and how you can use this information to help others which, in turn, helps you.

AMY

In Mark W. Schaefer's book, *Return on Influence*, he writes: "In the world of influence marketing, Amy (Howell) is a superconnector," (Page 17, Chapter 2 on "Igniting Epidemics"). What is a superconnector? According to Mark, it is someone who can convince and convert behaviors in real life through an online influence. You will have to read his book to learn more about what businesses are doing with this information, and how online influence is driving business strategies. As a high gear career seeker, it would be valuable to understand the key principles in his book.

Making connections with people—influential in your immediate circle or outside your circle—can lead to high gear career building. Connecting the dots for me means understanding what my clients' goals are, finding people in the market to help them reach their goals, and introducing them to one another. It can be like matchmaking—finding a need and matching it with someone who can meet that need.

One of the stories I share often was a significant career-changing connection which happened early in my career, in 1992. A CEO of a transportation company wanted to play golf at Augusta National. During a meeting he told me that was a lifelong dream of his. At that time, I worked for a real estate company with a good connection to Augusta National—one of its founders. Determined to help this CEO fulfill his dream, I arranged a meeting with the member of the exclusive golf club and this CEO. It took some creativity and persistence, but I convinced the founder to have lunch and meet this CEO. I reserved a private room at a well-known restaurant as a strategy for conducting a productive meeting. We had a delicious lunch, and at the right time, I put the issue squarely on the table. I turned to the golf club member and said, "Mr. Jones (that's not his real name) has a lifelong dream of playing golf at Augusta National, and he would offer to fly anyone in his private jet to play golf there anytime if he could participate." It was a high gear discussion and the two not only played that golf game, but many more following. I was acting as the superconnector for the CEO. And to this day, that lunch ranks as one of the most high gear lunches I've ever brokered.

The important back story is how I met the CEO in the first place. I was probably 25 or 26, and I met him on a legislative meet-and-greet trip our chamber of commerce took to Nashville. As a chamber volunteer, I had raised the most money out of our young leaders' membership development team, so I won a seat on this coveted trip where the chamber took only board members, local elected officials, and power players. Here I was, low woman on the chain of corporate structure, and by far the youngest, getting a plane ride to Nashville with Memphis' top movers, shakers, and leaders.

A week prior to the trip, I requested an advance copy of the list of people attending. I studied the bios of the board members and other attendees. I knew some of them, but I had certainly not worked directly with many of them. The CEO sat next to me on that flight. Admittedly, a bit of luck. I seized the opportunity to begin a conversation. Yes, it was intimidating, but being in high gear means overcoming fear and moving forward anyway. By the time we landed, this CEO knew more about me, and I knew that he was incoming chairman of the chamber board of directors. By making the most of this opportunity, I captured 30 minutes of one-on-one conversation—not an easy feat to accomplish with a C-level.

Our group toured the state capitol and met with state legislators. On the return flight, I boarded and the CEO asked the person seated next to me if she would mind changing seats so he could discuss business with me. He asked me to consider working for their organization and to apply for a number of positions at the company. His firm was about to go public and things were looking great for this company's future. I thanked him, and told him I would consider the offer. I later wrote him a letter thanking him for the opportunity and welcomed him to contact me in the future.

About two weeks later, I received a phone call from his Human Resources Director. She asked me to come in for an interview which I did but later declined a position with that company. While it was awesome to be wanted (and the pay was better), I was only in my second year working for a national CPA firm, and I wanted to finish what I was building at that firm. This is how I connected the dots to the CEO!

Once I had impressed this CEO with my chamber fundraising and high gear conversations, he remembered me, took my phone calls, and when I needed a CEO recommendation for Leadership Memphis, he was glad to write a letter for me. It is that type of connecting that can happen when you are working in high gear. Had I not been volunteering—in my spare time—for the chamber of commerce, I would never have met the decision makers I met at that point early in my career. Later, connecting dots with those people and others was a way to leverage deeper connections not only for myself but also my clients and organizations I worked with. It may have been my high gear work that led to early career success, but it was definitely the dot-connecting that prepared me to start my own firm at the age of 30.

There are new dot-connecting strategies through the many social media tools we have today. LinkedIn is a great research tool for people at all levels and types of organizations to connect dots.

However, there is tremendous power in real-life connections. Dot-connecting success depends on meeting people, communicating information, and helping them achieve their goals. This also requires building a network of business associates and contacts. In the *Foreword*, FedEx's Mike Glenn noted that one way to do this is through getting involved in a not-for-profit where you can meet other dot connectors. Graduates should practice the soft skills of face-to-face conversations including maintaining eye contact and a firm handshake. There is no substitute for quality in-person conversation. In every business encounter, ask questions and listen.

Knowledge is powerful; you'll be surprised how much can be gleaned from a first-person conversation void of emoticons and assumptions.

ANNE

Dot-connecting is the fancy term for making friendships in business and being genuinely interested in other people. You can't pretend to be genuine, especially online, because people can tell if you're selling or if you're engaging. Because I started my public relations firm at age 40, after staying home raising our three sons for 15 years, I had some serious dot-connecting to do to catch up to my peers. And I didn't have the luxury of 20 years to figure out the art of entrepreneurship and doing business. I had to find the most influential, most experienced business people I knew and ask them to be on my personal board of advisors.

My story about Jillian, the high school senior who was my intern, is the perfect illustration of dot-connecting. She saw an opportunity and connected the dots to an introduction to me and then secured an internship. There is no magic bullet to this process, and it is no respecter of status, race, position, gender, or earning power. As you advance your career, you will reach high gear sooner if you begin to introduce yourself to influential people and superconnectors. During college you'll be establishing in-person connections and simultaneously building your online community. You will need them both to build your personal brand.

Who are some of the superconnectors you should build a relationship with? Start on your campus:

1. Does the president of the University know who you are? If not, schedule an appointment to introduce yourself. Make sure his or her Admin knows who you are. Attend an event where he/she is speaking and then live tweet it using the event hashtag.
2. Do your professors know your name and your career goals?

3. Do your parents' business colleagues know your career goals? Have you sought their advice at all? The 50-year-old business executives are reaching half-time in their careers. They are looking for younger people to invest in, to share the wisdom of experience. Lucky you if you can be that recipient of hard-won knowledge.

4. Do the executives you do business with know your career goals: the president of the bank you use, your physician, your dentist, the owner of the car dealership, your deans? You should introduce yourself to each of these people and stay in contact with them. They can advance your career.

5. When the college or business community needs a volunteer, are you first on their list? When a young person is sitting at a township meeting, a non-profit board meeting, a school board meeting, a college press conference, you stand out. Be the young person who is memorable for your earnestness, your willingness to jump in and help, and your leadership skills. Be well-informed.

A great way to begin to make a name for yourself and be noticed by superconnectors is to write an editorial or Letter to the Editor for your regional or college newspaper. If you have an unusual experience with a topic, go higher gear and submit it to a national newspaper like *The Wall Street Journal*. And although students now are considered digital natives, the power of print is not dead. *The Wall Street Journal* has the largest print circulation in the U.S. with 2.2 million subscribers and a digital audience of 36 million per month. Being published in print or online helps increase your network and your digital tattoo.

One of my good friends, Kim Ortenzio-Nielsen, is a consummate superconnector. When she walks into a room, you know it. She has an infectious, bubbly personality, and a spirit of helpfulness. She serves on several boards and committees and is well-known for getting things done. Her husband, Dr. Bob Nielsen, tells a funny story of an event they attended in New York. Bob is a physician, and a leading authority on electronic medical records and population health. When they walked into the room, Kim noticed someone that she knew. "In a different state, at a physician's event, Kim finds somebody that knows her. Why am I not surprised?" says Bob.

Because she is highly connected, Kim is often in a fundraising leadership position—a role that most people don't want to volunteer for because they feel uncomfortable and awkward asking for money. High gear people can be found doing hard jobs that no one else wants.

If you want to find who the influencers are in any community, volunteer for a fundraising position. If your college is doing a capital campaign or a development drive, volunteer. You'll meet leaders on your campus, and you'll meet leaders in the community. The type of business executives who are being approached for donations are the very people who can help you connect with companies who are hiring.

When you sit on these committees, you learn about the business fabric of a community. You learn who the philanthropists are, who sits on foundation boards, and you will have the opportunity to meet with them. Even if all you do is listen and do much-needed but simple tasks like getting office supplies or making copies of documents, you begin to see how the engine of business churns. And that's extremely valuable to preparing for your future high gear.

Be strategic. If you volunteer for a committee with The Salvation Army, and you volunteer to be on their Event Committee, or in charge of a Red Kettle Campaign, then you have a reason to schedule meetings with business leaders. You have an opportunity to invite them to donate to your cause or listen to your event sponsorship request. In these conversations, you'll start to learn and practice persuasion skills and negotiating skills.

For example, let's say you are on the American Heart Association (AHA) Go Red committee. Use your research skills learned in college to get a grasp on why people, and in particular, businesses, should care about heart disease. Heart disease is the No. 1 killer of women in the U.S. Keeping employees healthy is a business advantage. You've just asked a corporate partner to donate $5,000 for the AHA walk-a-thon in your city. They tell you that they've already committed $2,500 for Community Fund X. You can use this opportunity to shift into high gear statistician mode and share the facts about heart disease and stroke.

You would say that 1 in 3 American women will die from cardiovascular disease; that heart disease and stroke are the most preventable forms of death; and then share a regional statistic. Breast cancer awareness is always in the media spotlight and even the NFL wears pink cleats in October. When a young lady working for AHA told me that 67% of people in our three-county region will die from heart disease and/or stroke, but less than 1% in our region will die from breast cancer, that really was a powerful statistic.

Being well-informed, regardless of your age, shows executives and leaders that you are confident enough and smart enough to get in the ring of business. Don't let your age prevent you from seeking and earning a seat at the non-profit table or for-profit board table. Find the superconnectors and show them that you have something to say. When you develop these relationships at age 25, you're well on your way to high gear.

Building your online community begins with the quality of content you share. Attend social media conferences so you can be found in an event conversation and in the hashtag stream. Tweet during any meetings or events you attend so you're easily found online. Start a social media group at your college, and be the founder. These are stepping stones to gaining social influence. Based on your major or career, search for topics that interest you and find the influencers and follow them on social media.

If you're writing an opinion editorial or a blog post, reach out to your online influencers and ask them for an interview. If you are attending any type of conference, ask the panelists for a 90-second interview where you ask them a few questions and then post the content on YouTube. When you do this, you're developing your own social influence and sharing valuable information with your community.

I attended a Ragan Communications event in Las Vegas a few years ago and the speaker lineup was amazing. It was a social media conference and Colonel Douglas Wheelock was a speaker. Doug is a NASA astronaut who was the Commander of the International Space Station. He was the first astronaut to check in from space using Foursquare. His tweets and commentary as @Astro_Wheels were incredible. I asked him after he spoke if I could video him and ask a few questions. He is an influencer and was very excited to share his insights on social media and NASA. I videotaped our interview, and it's still receiving views today.

Just last week, I reached out to Colonel Wheelock on Twitter, in a Direct Message, to invite him to speak and be honored at our Salvation Army Harrisburg Capital City Region annual event. Your online superconnections can enrich your career and business relationships for years to come.

You are learning to create content like the media and share all the great stories you're learning with your online community. Stay current on regional and global news and connect with reporters and book authors. Share their content, and write comments on their blogs. That's how you build your community and begin to make powerful superconnections.

CHAPTER 10
Actions Speak Louder Than Words

"Visions without actions are hallucinations."

MICHAEL J. KAMI

Attaining success for our clients means actionable, results-driven work. Emphasis on work. Our clients value us, hire us, seek our professional counsel, and act on our recommendations because we have proven ourselves in deed and in reputation. Success doesn't magically appear to us—or to anyone—on a silver platter. Students, high gear action means setting your goals, and then acting daily to reach them.

AMY

One compelling statement I heard and never forgot is from Michael Kami: "Visions without actions are hallucinations." Mr. Kami was instrumental in launching IBM and Xerox. Later, he helped reenergize Harley-Davidson. While serving on the Rhodes College management speaker series committee, we selected Mr. Kami to speak to an audience of 300 business leaders. He was the most intelligent and inspiring speaker I had ever heard. I took notes on everything he said and later transcribed them for future reference. I still have those notes and every now and then I read them.

When Mr. Kami made that statement, something in my brain clicked. I thought to myself, "Yes, that's it! That's what most people miss." The problem with a plan—no matter how good it looks or reads—is that most of the time it is not executed. You can talk all day about what you want to do, and what you are going to do. It's quite different to actually do it. That's what Kami meant. High gear means doing, moving, forward thinking in action, accomplishing, finishing, improving, and continuously learning.

If you are going to be successful in college, work, and life, you will have to act and constantly look for ways to move forward in every situation. Some actions are more challenging than others. Doing nothing is not a high gear strategy; and in business, if you are not moving forward, you are falling behind.

High gear for college graduates means being an informed communicator and executer of positive actions for the job. If you are in sales, and you have a quota you have to meet, high gear says exceed that number. If you have a problem in your job that you don't know how to resolve, find a mentor or someone more experienced to help you figure it out.

Business owners depend on employees to be problem-solvers. If your boss or supervisor asks you to do a task, don't turn around and ask for a playbook. Those who independently and creatively navigate their way to solutions and positive outcomes are in demand. Businesses are not created to be teachers.

As an employer, I often see college graduates shy away from an unfamiliar task rather than learn how to complete it. In past employee reviews, I have pointed out that one must learn some of the tasks on the job description before they can be promoted. Don't ask your boss for a pay increase or additional time off if you are ignoring some of the duties in your job description. Further, if you aren't doing everything you can to master what is on that description, you may be replaced.

One day one of our young employees, let's call her Sabrina, received a review she wasn't happy about. We had tried to work with her and help her, but she refused to do things a certain way; she made mistakes often, recorded messages inaccurately. She could not spell, made basic grammatical errors, and repeated mistakes. We had

had enough. Shortly following this review—she was on notice that we were monitoring her performance—Sabrina came into my office with a list of new demands. She wanted me, her boss, to review her list and discuss it. Anyone with any amount of common sense would know this is the wrong approach. Sabrina's last day at my firm was the day she issued her list. Don't be Sabrina!

It is never easy to terminate an employee, and although I have had to do it, it's not something I have ever grown used to. The truth is most employees fire themselves. If you don't actually do your job well, you should not expect to keep it. Companies need employees that contribute greatness in skill, talent, leadership, and a positive attitude.

We also talk often in business about employees who spin their wheels—people who seem busy, but don't accomplish much. I had another employee once who had a decent attitude, but took forever to get work out the door. Often her response to me when asked about the status of work was, "Oh, that's pending in my Outbox." What? High gear people don't have drafts piling up in their Outbox. Try to anticipate your teacher or boss. If I have to ask my team for a status report, that means either the work is not being done quickly enough, or someone isn't communicating the progress.

Stay ahead and communicate progress often. This might mean working a few hours at night to catch up. Arrive early for meetings and interviews. Sometimes "on time" can be considered late. One day this same employee with drafts in her Outbox showed up to a client meeting five minutes late carrying a cup of Starbucks coffee—for her, not for anyone else. If you are running late, don't stop and get coffee. And if you do stop for coffee, bring some for everyone and don't be late.

Here are some actionable work tips:

1. Be organized in your communications. For example, if you are in a group email, and your supervisor is copied, don't reply to each person's email. Business people are busy, and

we don't want to be barraged by emails. I recommend preparing a list of questions and needs and delivering these in one concise email update. Know when to email versus when to call.

2. Think before you act. My first boss told me "Amy, haste makes waste. Slow down and make sure you are checking your work." This advice came following some mortifying errors I had made in a document.

3. Verify your work and fact-check it before you present. Have someone else review the assignment, and ask for constructive comments.

4. Get ahead on email early in the day and complete as many administrative tasks as possible in the morning, so you can focus on work that generates results and revenue throughout the day.

5. Plan your work, and work your plan. Early in my career I had a boss who taught me to plan your next week out—specifically list what you need to get done.

6. Understand the differences between A, B, and C tasks. This means understanding what the most important actionable tasks are, and do them first. Most people fill their day doing the easy C tasks first. Is answering an ad representative's email more important than setting up a client meeting? Tackle your most challenging assignments first.

Superconnector Mark W. Schaefer (@MarkWSchaefer, see pg. 118) is a blogger, author, marketing consultant, and faculty member at Rutgers University where he teaches marketing through social media and blogging. He is arguably one of the world's top experts on blogging for business and travels the globe speaking. Mark is a perfect example of the powerful connections you can make online. I met Mark on Twitter six years ago and when a client meeting landed me in his hometown of Knoxville, Tennessee, I called him and asked for an in-person meeting. We were immediate friends who shared a passion for social media and marketing. I am now proud to say he is part of my inner circle or crew that I rely on for advice, information, and connections. Mark shares his advice on high gear job searching:

I'm fortunate that I get to speak to a lot of college classes, and I am often asked for tips on how to stand out in today's job market. My response may surprise you: Build a personal brand through a blog!

You might think of blogs as places to find product reviews or maybe follow your favorite brand. But a personal blog can also be a very strategic tool to help you stand out in a crowded marketplace. **In fact, there are seven reasons every job seeker should blog.**

1. **Show what you're made of.** In an interview, you normally have to try to convince people that you know what you know. In a blog, you can SHOW them. Blog about current events in your industry, your view on trends and developments, and demonstrate your areas of expertise.

2. **Build a professional network.** There are lots of examples where people found jobs through connections in a blog community. Recently I helped connect a young woman into the professional marketing scene in Chicago, because I was impressed with her blog. Your blog community can certainly become a professional network.

3. **Engaging versus advertising.** Let's face it. No matter how creative you get, a resume is still an advertisement. I struggle with reading through a lengthy resume; however, I will read interesting stories on a blog all day long. Compelling content engages prospective employers in a way that will hold their attention.

4. **Point of differentiation.** In today's world, blogging may be an expectation of many entry-level jobs, especially if you are

going into sales, marketing, public relations, or human resources. Demonstrating an ability to create content may just be the difference that gets you the job.

5. **Sharpen your professional skills.** If you're going to blog about a subject, you need to know your stuff. Putting out thoughtful content requires that you stay on top of your game, which will certainly be an advantage to you, especially if the job-hunting process is a long one.

6. **Expand your reach.** Building your personal brand means showing up in all the places a prospective employer might find you. Of course that usually means LinkedIn. But having a link to a blog on your profile, as well as displaying a feed of your recent blog posts, gives a potential employer reviewing your LinkedIn profile more ways to connect with you and learn about your skills.

7. **Extend the interview.** Here is the last thing you say to your interviewer: "I've enjoyed our time together but there is so much more I could tell you about my abilities. I hope you'll take a look at my blog (the web address is on my resume) so you can see for yourself the way I think about things." And you know what? They'll do it. You have just extended your interview by another 15–30 minutes and that may make all the difference!

Here's one last high gear tip for using a personal blog strategically.

A few years ago, I interviewed for an executive position in New York. The job description listed five key elements of the job. A week before the interview, I wrote five blog posts on each of those elements and posted them each day leading up to my interview. When my interviewers read my blog, they were amazed to see how closely aligned my skills were to the job requirements!

To benefit from all of Mark's insight, read his blog at www.BusinessGrow.com and order his books: *The Tao of Twitter*, *Return on Influence*, *Social Media Explained*, and his latest, *The Content Code*.

ANNE

College is a time for learning, but very soon you'll be thrust into a world of expectations and deliverables. Employers and organizations are looking for people who can get things done. Politics is probably the only area where a decade can pass without any forward progress or goals met, and people still get paid.

As you prepare to enter the workforce, make sure you understand how money is made in business. It's important to understand how particular businesses generate revenue—law firms and ad agencies bill by time increments; manufacturing firms bill by product orders; real estate professionals bill by percentages of selling price/listing price; banks earn fees for services; building owners lease by square feet; PR firms bill by the hour or by pitch and placements.

When you are interviewing, and you understand how the potential employer makes money, you can market yourself and your value-add to the company. What skills are you bringing to the marketplace that makes a company more intelligent, more competitive, more efficient, or more newsworthy?

High gear students take initiatives, and ask to help out regardless of compensation. By that I mean, if your firm is just returning to profitability after the recession, and they had to cut several positions, look to help out in any of the roles that were eliminated or curtailed. Marketing and PR were certainly two of those areas. Young people bring a social media savvy that older workers haven't been exposed to. You understand the tools, and we employers have the wisdom of business experience. Combined, the two make a formidable marketing powerhouse.

I recently had the privilege of judging a college business plan competition called the Impact Venture Challenge. It was an inaugural event at Messiah College and the teams had to create and launch a business that would demonstrate profitability and impact a community or group of people for social good. The concept was brilliant, and Brian Nejmeh, the professor of entrepreneurship, was amazed at how many teams applied. I was incredibly impressed with the scope of creativity, their passion for making a difference, and the students' fearlessness to jump in to tackle complex issues.

After three rounds of Shark Tank-like examinations and eliminations, the final challenge culminated in six teams presenting to a panel of six executive and academic judges in front of a packed audience. I was thrilled that these young people were learning such marketable skills at the young ages of 19 and 20. They had to think through their idea critically, research processes and procedures, create a balance sheet, predict profit and loss, calculate a risk/benefit analysis, develop a marketing plan, and then sell the idea to the judges and the community in a live presentation.

After I accepted the invitation to judge the Impact Venturists, I familiarized myself with the competition by watching the pitch YouTube video that introduced the Challenge to students on campus and invited them to participate. The interviewer posed the question: "Have you ever thought about starting a business?" The students were intrigued by the idea of combining entrepreneurship and social good and honest in their answers. I confess that when I was in college, I never imagined nor aspired to owning my own business; and I certainly didn't understand the private-public sectors, or the effects of the GDP on the economy.

This challenge was about starting a business with a higher calling. The requirement was that it had to be profitable and sustainable, as well as impactful. In the video, when asked the questions, some of the students said: "I don't have that business mindset. I don't have that type of business mind. I have thought about it, but I'm in college." The one that left the biggest impression on me was a young lady who said, "I admittedly have maybe an unfairly negative view of the concept of business."

Perhaps a lot of college students hold that opinion, or they have a discolored view of "Wall Street" and its influence on small business. The first step to correcting the negative concept is education and experiencing a start-up first-hand is baptism by fire.

The positive value of business to a college is unmistakable. On a college campus, look at the names on your business schools, the science centers, the dorms, the library, the stadium. Consider the hospitals, the research centers, the churches, the day cares, the YWCAs. All funded by successful people who were good at business and could in turn donate to the non-profits who take care of community needs.

Those students who reach high gear understand the mutually beneficial relationship between businesses and the communities they support. The great news is that everyone in the audience of the Impact Venture Challenge now understands clearly the value, power, and capacity to impact societal change through business.

Penn State University President Dr. Eric Barron is a proponent of every college student having the opportunity to minor in business regardless of major. Students need to understand how the economy churns. The more young people who graduate with an understanding of the GDP, the power of small business as an economic driver, and what quarterly job reports mean, the quicker they reach high gear in any chosen industry.

CHAPTER 11

Building Excellence in Students Begins with a Presidential Vision

"It's not about you—it's about Who can you serve?"

DR. BOB FISHER

Our pièce de résistance for *Students in High Gear* is "A Presidential Vision," which reveals the DNA behind the institutional leadership of several university and college CEOs. University presidents are always in high gear. They are the face of their institutional brand, and a combination of business executive, visionary, and servant leader.

Dr. Bob Fisher is all of those attributes and many more. As the president of Belmont, he is passionate and excited about providing the best environment to allow every Belmont student to achieve a path to high gear. He believes Belmont is educating the kind of spirited young people who will change the world. He shared his vision and insight with us.

What Makes Belmont a High Gear University?
Dr. Bob Fisher, President, Belmont University, Nashville, Tennessee

Belmont University has been in high gear for the past 15 years. In 2000, the university enrolled 2,976 students and by 2014 that number had risen to 7,318 with the average ACT rising from 24.5 to 26.5. The phenomenal growth in student enrollment has been accompanied by more than doubling faculty and staff numbers to over 1,000 and investing more than $500 million in new campus construction.

At the same time, we have been able to double faculty and staff salaries as the university budget increased from $38 million to $212 million. New programs have been added including a College of Law, a School of Pharmacy, and several undergraduate majors.

By any measure Belmont has truly experienced transformational change. But almost paradoxically, what has enabled all of the above to be radically changed is something that has not changed and, in fact, seems to be more deeply entrenched than ever. And that is the mission and values of the university.

Communicating the mission, vision, and values of the university begins with describing "What Belmont believes about you" in the very earliest communications with prospective students and continues throughout the time that the students call Belmont home.

Belmont believes that every student was created by God for a unique purpose. Everyone is on this Earth for a reason. It has been said that the two most important days in a person's life are the day of their birth and the day they discover their purpose in life.

And Belmont doesn't think God would create a person for a unique reason, and then just wish them good luck and sit back and be a spectator in their lives. Instead, God has given each student the talent, abilities, passions, and other gifts that they need to achieve their unique purpose.

The good news is that every freshman who arrives at Belmont brings everything they need in order to live out their purpose. The more challenging yet still really good news is that they will have to put in the 10,000 hours of work that Malcolm Gladwell talks about in his book *Outliers* if they want to uncover and develop their talents, abilities, and passions to fully become the person they were created to be.

This time in college is one of the greatest gifts that anyone can receive if they use the time to discover the purpose of their lives and to fully develop their gifts. While the university is not able to assign purpose to students, it does seek to create an environment where purpose can be discovered and refined.

The best hint that the university gives to students regarding their purpose is to tell them "It's not about you—it's about Who can you serve?" The greatest privilege anyone can ever have in life is to be in a position to help someone, and when one's purpose is matched with a need in the world, the result is a meaningful and joyful life.

It's this hope and this commitment that has kept Belmont in High Gear, and will keep it moving forward.

Dr. Eric J. Barron is the 18th president of Penn State University and assumed the position in May 2014. An accomplished scientist with a long history of geological and atmospheric research experience, Dr. Barron brings high gear vision to PSU students. "These are times of opportunity, and we must move forward strategically. We must innovate. We must prioritize. We must continue to think boldly," states the University's Strategic Plan.

Just what goals does he have for this world-renowned institution? Like Dr. Fisher, he shared his personal insights on the community of students he serves.

A Full Speed Ahead Future
Dr. Eric J. Barron, President, Pennsylvania State University,
State College, Pennsylvania

As one of the nation's 31 million students enrolled in college or as a recent graduate—congratulations! Earning a degree is one of the best choices you can make on your way to career success and lifelong learning. It is, however, only one step, and it needs to be a part of a plan to take full advantage of the breadth and depth of opportunities available in college and beyond. As the coach Yogi Berra said, "You got to be careful if you don't know where you're going, because you might not get there."

As part of the direction offered in this book, I would like to share two pieces of advice that I hope you'll find useful on the open road ahead.

First, I'd like you to think about college (and your early career/ post-college years) as a version of America's sports car—perhaps a blue and white sports car. When you get into the driver's seat, you have a choice. You can drive that car at 20 miles per hour, or you can put that sports car through its paces—in high gear—to see what it can do, and to see how far it can go. Which do you choose?

The same goes for college and your career. You can just go to class, or you can maximize the experience by being fully engaged in everything you do. Seek out academic, research, learning, and athletic opportunities—follow your interests and explore them. Always consider what's important to you and pursue worthwhile activities as they arise. And if you have a particular interest, find out early what you have to do to be ready. If you do so, I guarantee that you will be happier, make better choices, have stronger resumes, and more successful careers.

So, this is a key opportunity—the opportunity to see how far you can take your education and your ambition. If you do that, there will be incredibly positive outcomes for you.

I realize that some of you are just starting out: you haven't even settled on a major, let alone planned for an internship, research project, or career. But it's never too early to start thinking about your goals. Some of the decisions you make will have a great impact on options available to you later.

There are people at universities who can help you identify choices and advise you as to the consequences of certain alternatives. Talk to them. Many career services offices will continue to help you long after you have earned your diploma— stay in touch! At Penn State, our network of more than 600,000 living alumni is indispensable for career advice and networking possibilities.

This brings me to one last story I like to tell about learning to drive a car with my father. It was an experience of constantly correcting and over-correcting as I tried to steer the car. My father said, "Eric, instead of driving by looking at the hood ornament, lift up your head and look down the road; you will discover it is much easier to get where you want to go."

Your family, friends, colleagues, and your university's faculty and staff are ready to help you see down the road, to sense the future, and to find success. I urge you to start every day in high gear and to seize the opportunities ahead. Best wishes, and enjoy the ride!

Transforming the student experience at Central Penn College to meet today's career needs, Dr. Karen M. Scolforo brings industry, private and public sector voices, and executives to the curriculum table. She says, "We partner with community leaders to develop the most relevant programs for our students and to make sure we continuously deliver a career-focused education. Every course we offer ultimately impacts the training and employability of our more than 6,500 graduates."

Dr. Scolforo is the ninth president of Central Penn College, founded in Summerdale, Pennsylvania in 1881, and she is an enthusiastic advocate for providing students with every tool and opportunity to reach high gear.

Dr. Karen M. Scolforo, President, Central Penn College, Summerdale, Pennsylvania

Amy D. Howell and Anne Deeter Gallaher are onto something big in *Students in High Gear*. Now more than ever, responsibility and accountability are critical to career success. We know that industry professionals want to hire college graduates who are prepared to hit the ground running. Not only must these graduates have the necessary technical skills to compete in their chosen fields, but they must also demonstrate the soft skills to promote positive working relationships, develop partnerships, and employ the necessary verbal and written communication skills to convey important ideas and concepts.

In today's economy, institutions of higher education have the added responsibility of preparing graduates to meet the needs of employers. The most effective way to do this is to the develop industry partnerships in advance, to allow business leaders to write and review curriculum, and to ensure that faculty receive the necessary professional development to offer cutting-edge, hands-on experiences in the classroom and beyond. These partnerships extend to middle schools and secondary schools as we work together to align curriculum and create a seamless educational experience.

Central Penn College traces its roots to 1881 and includes a rich history of career development and advancement. In the past year, over 88% of our graduates either earned positions in their chosen fields or pursued advanced degrees. All Central Penn College students engage in hands-on learning, internship opportunities or capstone projects, and service requirements as our highly credentialed and experienced faculty prepare them for the workplace.

We incorporate the Practice of Professionalism in all of our classes so that students gain valuable soft skills. Our Career Services department offers lifetime career placement assistance and continually demonstrates a strong commitment to student success, regardless if a student completes an associate's, bachelor's, or master's degree.

Several times a year Central Penn College invites industry professionals to our campus to assess our curriculum, textbooks, materials, and laboratories. Elicited feedback is taken seriously and used for continual improvement.

Employers commend Central Penn College for our success in preparing our students for their careers. Most of the advisement we receive relates to industry changes, modified expectations, and technical advancement. Employers want to see strong writing skills, so we developed a writing center, and more than 70% of our students take advantage of this during their programs, and especially during finals week.

We are continually upgrading our technology centers and improving our online platform, as well as our ground and hybrid programming. For our students, information is available at their fingertips.

We continue to expand our program offerings as a direct response to workforce and community needs, such as our recently approved bachelor degrees in Radiology Sciences, Healthcare Management, and Health Sciences. Students are invited to participate in poetry slams, town hall meetings, athletics, and service events, such as fundraising walks/runs and days of caring. We opened our Cultural Diversity Center and reached out to our global community in 2014. We continue to travel to other countries across the globe to collaborate and connect on career opportunities.

To graduate and launch high gear students, our 2016–2020 strategic plan is focused on student learning, growth initiatives, branding, and financial stability. We expect to expand our reach across the globe and our graduates will continue to exceed employer needs. The future of Central Penn College graduates is bright, and we look forward to serving the needs of our partners and community for a long time to come.

Community colleges are a powerful gateway to completing a college degree and achieving a new frontier of career opportunities. Led by a president who joined Twitter in 2011 and has shared more than 11,500 tweets about the value of a #HACC education, Harrisburg Area Community College is a workforce treasure in central Pennsylvania.

Dr. John Sygielski, or Ski, as he is affectionately known, became the seventh president of HACC, Central Pennsylvania's Community College, in July 2011. He was president of Mt. Hood Community College in Gresham, Oregon, and president of Lord Fairfax Community College in Middletown, Virginia.

Ski is a member of the American Association of Community Colleges' (AACC) 21st-Century Commission on the Future of Community Colleges and is a past chairman of AACC's board. He is chairman of the National Community College Advisory Council, which advises Education Testing Service on their products and services for community colleges.

The only member of his working-class family to graduate from college, Ski is an author, speaker, and former adjunct business faculty member. Most importantly, he is passionate about opening paths to high gear for every learner.

A Community College in High Gear
Dr. John "Ski" Sygielski, President, HACC, Central Pensylvania's Community College, Harrisburg, Pennsylvania

Vibrant communities need education and innovation hubs. And one of the most powerful centers of influence for a city, as well as an economic driver, is a community college. More than half of all U.S. undergraduate students are enrolled in our 11,000 community colleges, which are critical for workforce training and retraining. HACC, Central Pennsylvania's Community College, enrolls approximately 20,000 students from 10 central Pennsylvania counties on five campuses and through our Virtual Learning offerings.

Compared to a four-year college or university, community colleges such as HACC provide at least four important advantages for students: 1. It's easy to enroll, regardless of prior academic records; 2. Lower fees and tuition; 3. An open admission policy; and, 4. A more flexible curriculum and class schedule. HACC achieves this while still maintaining its focus on the academic rigor of our programs that we know is key to our students' successes.

Most of the students at HACC come to the college with a wide range of educational and career goals. HACC's students, like many community college students, come to the institution for at least three reasons: 1. To obtain certification in certain occupational fields; 2. To obtain an associate's degree; or 3. To gain academic experience and prepare for a four-year institution of higher learning.

To ensure HACC students and, more importantly, HACC graduates are well prepared for the ever-changing global workplace, we engage employers in conversations about their changing workforce needs and integrate their comments and recommendations into our credit and non-credit courses and programs. It is through our engagement with employers—our ground truth—that we can be the region's first choice for a quality and accessible education.

Our mission is to create opportunities and transform lives to shape the future. For over 50 years we have been dedicated to that mission and nearly 750,000 individuals in our communities can attest to the difference it has made in their professional and personal lives. It's HACC's privilege to continue to expand educational experiences and prepare every student for a game-changing high gear.

Dr. M. David Rudd, named president of University of Memphis (UofM) in 2014, brings 30 years of experience to his presidency and is focused on all aspects of the university. He applies strategic and innovative solutions in the changing landscape of academics, financials, development, community relations, research, and athletics. One of Dr. Rudd's most important issues is clearly student success. His passion for seeing students graduate and move into the workforce is evident in every conversation and presentation. Under his leadership, freshman applications have increased by 186% and fundraising has reached a record level during his first year as president, exceeding $37 million. He shares his thoughts on the strength of student potential.

Dr. M. David Rudd, President, University of Memphis (UofM), Memphis, Tennessee

Given the array of challenges today's college students must balance, the vast majority are in high gear the entirety of their time on campus. In past years, students may have had a year or two to ease into college life. That's not the case today. With rapidly escalating costs and declining state support, the issue of balancing work and school is paramount, coupled with the demands of achieving a balanced, comprehensive educational experience that improves the odds of a job or post-graduate work.

I am consistently amazed at the ability of students at the University of Memphis to successfully navigate this demanding landscape, with time-management, innovative thinking, creativity, flexibility, and an entrepreneurial spirit proving critical to successful outcomes.

Students in high gear are able to achieve a comprehensive educational experience, regardless of major; one that provides the skills, knowledge base, and life perspective critical to eventual employment or post-graduate work. Perhaps more than any time in history, applied experience is essential for today's graduates. The number of students that transition from internship or co-op placements to their first full-time career opportunity is stunningly high.

Students in high gear find a way to integrate applied experiences into their degree pathway. Those wanting to move on to post-graduate work find a way to engage in on-campus research labs. In short, students in high gear don't hesitate to take advantage of opportunities. They don't shrink from challenge or disappointment. They're creative, flexible, and arguably most important, persistent.

One last characteristic is worth mentioning about students in high gear. Those that are ultimately the most successful recognize the importance of networking early in college and are able to develop and refine this skill as they move through their curriculum. They understand that life is about relationships, regardless of talent or intellectual capacity. Our world is a social one. Success is about people, it's about being able to connect, relate, and communicate in the written and spoken word.

The challenges faced by today's college students are many, but the quality of instruction is unparalleled, the pace of change unprecedented, and the opportunities limited only by one's imagination.

CHAPTER 12

High Gear Professors and How to Connect with Them

"An investment in knowledge always pays the best interest."

BEN FRANKLIN

The call to arms for big ideas, passionate workers, and an energized economy depends on university leaders who inspire and challenge the next generation. We believe—now more than anytime in our U.S. history—teaching our youth should be an honored and respected responsibility. And we are grateful for the high gear excellence of our higher ed professionals who have contributed to our book.

AMY

One of the most inspiring and educational aspects of writing this book was talking with so many college professors and faculty. When some of the accomplished people in this book understood our premise, what we were seeking to share, and why we wanted to write this book, they were equally passionate about participating.

We're grateful for the positive influence teachers have on our children. Many of us are in successful careers today because of the investment and support of a dedicated teacher. To provide a complete picture of higher ed, we sought the passionate input from teachers and professors who share our spirit of intentional, high gear goal-setting. We love what they have to say about the beginnings and foundations of their education principles.

Jason M. Keith, Interim Dean, Bagley College of Engineering, Mississippi State University

A university education provides a great background of the technical topics students need to be successful. However, this is just the tip of the iceberg. These fundamentals will stay with you as you build project upon project, and success upon success. There are a few things I would like to highlight as being critically important as you work in your careers, or to focus on as you take the final steps to graduation.

The first is being part of a team. I was involved in team projects in school, both formally and informally, and have had to work to develop my teaming skills. The demands of being a strong team player are even harder on you today. You will be asked to be part of teams with members that you will never meet, in places that you will never visit, on projects where your experience is needed.

Keep open communication within your team. I cannot stress this enough. If you don't communicate, then nobody really knows what is going on in your project, or within your organization. Talk often to the people that you directly work with, daily if needed. Interact on a regular basis with those under you and with those who are above you.

Another important rule that you should follow in being on a team is to not be afraid to ask for help. For many of you this may be awkward, so it is best done by finding a mentor. When I was a student, I was involved in some research projects on computer modeling of the diffusion of semiconductor materials processes with fundamental applications for the computing industry. The position was off-campus so it was similar to an internship. It gave me the opportunity to be part of a unique team project, working with a professor from another university who was lead investigator of the research project. He was usually on campus, but did not visit the site where I worked. I suspect he was in touch often with other members of the team. I worked mainly with his post-doctoral researcher. Since I wanted to earn a Ph.D. and work as a university professor, I asked him many questions about graduate school. I also asked about the things that the professor did. Of course, I also learned about the technical aspects of the project, but just as importantly, I learned what to expect in my future. In addition, the place where I worked employed other graduate students on different projects, so I was also able to learn a lot of technical stuff by speaking with them, as well as the expectations that were upon them as students.

When you ask mentors these sorts of questions, you learn what is important to do. But you also learn what you should not do. In research, it is customary for some employers to assign you a formal mentor. This is good, but you should also find at least one on your own—someone that you will not be afraid to ask questions of. And remember that as time goes on you will need to find different mentors that can help you understand your present job.

As a graduate student, I spoke to graduates about the job search process. I found a mentor as a professor at Michigan Tech and have found new ones here at Mississippi State, with the goal of learning how to be an effective academic administrator in order to best represent my faculty, staff, and students.

Also, don't forget the people who work for you. Treat everyone as if they are the most important person in your organization. Find out what they are passionate about in their workplace, and think of how you can support them. As you bring new people on board, share your best tips for success with them just like your mentors have done with you. Also, greet them in their offices at least once a week, ask them how they are doing, and how their families are. Celebrate their successes.

Don't be afraid to learn new things, to make mistakes, and to learn from those mistakes. As an example, math is a powerful tool and helps you understand the physics of the engineering problem you may be trying to solve. There is always more than one way to find a solution. You all have the potential to teach yourself these new things. The combination of asking experts and mentors and getting the experience of knowing where to look and what to read is a skill that you will develop over the next few years.

There is one final area that has been helpful to me and requires constant work. That is to be organized. I always had a certain level of organization on the job and at home. However, several years ago I began a research project with a colleague who knew where everything was, and when you would ask him a question, he would answer very quickly. I changed my behaviors to be more like him. I began to do a better job in filing my project notes so I was equipped to answer rapidly. I have tried to use this skill in all aspects of my job and personal life. I also spend a few minutes each day putting things away where they belong. That saves time in searching for something.

In 10, 20, and 30 years, you will look back at the time you were in school. You may not think it now, but it will probably be the best time of your life. Why not make the most of it and set yourself up for success in high gear?

Justin Lawhead, Associate Dean, Student Leadership and Involvement, The University of Memphis

It is clear that leadership programs can contribute to the personal development of students, but what still may be missing is how those competencies can be translated to skills desired by employers.

A Gallup survey conducted on behalf of the Lumina Foundation found that only 11% of business leaders and only 14% of the general public felt strongly that students graduated from college with the skills and competencies that are needed for success in the workplace (Lumina, 2013).

In another study, Hart Research Associates interviewed 318 employers and found that both two- and four-year colleges need to make at least some improvements to prepare students for the global economy.

Clearly employers and the general public have lost confidence in the ability of colleges and universities to prepare students for the world of work. However, the University of Memphis Leadership Education and Development (LEAD) program is working to be a high gear university by bridging this gap through relationship building, community engagement, and active use of leaders within the greater Memphis community.

Local government, business, and nonprofit leaders have all identified a critical need for university graduates to enter our community with proven leadership ability. The University of Memphis LEAD program provides students with leadership training designed to help them succeed in the real world. LEAD students learn about problem solving, team building, critical thinking, and other essential skills for the future workplace. We challenge our students to dream, think, and do.

By working with community partners in the private and public sectors, LEAD provides students with important activities and programs to engage with professionals and discover what it means—and what it takes—to lead. Local leaders can tell their leadership stories and lessons and expose students to undiscovered opportunities through a program called *Lunch with a Leader*. This informal program brings students and high gear community leaders together to discuss a wide range of leadership topics. At the University of Memphis, we have discovered high-performing leaders are readily available and willing to engage with our students. They realize that building and sustaining a thriving community comes through cultivating and interacting with the next generation of leaders.

Our *Professional Connections Program* matches a select group of students with community leaders for guided conversations about professional and personal development. The primary goal is to give students a practical experience to establish a professional network for guidance and growth. Discussion subjects include personal branding, interviewing, and resume development. Professionals also have a first-hand opportunity to source talent for internships or entry-level positions.

The University of Memphis LEAD program is focused on career development as part of our training efforts. A high gear leadership program maximizes its programming through external community collaboration creating a comprehensive effort to educate and develop tomorrow's leaders.

Hart Research Associates (2013). It takes more than a major: Employer Priorities for College Learning. Liberal Education, 99(2), 22–29.

Lumina Foundation. (2013). The 2013 Lumina Study of the American Public's Opinion on Higher Education and U.S. Business Leader's Poll on Higher Education. Indianapolis, IN.

ANNE

I recently attended a President's Circle breakfast presented by the Harrisburg Regional Chamber of Commerce. It is an invitation-only event with executives, decision makers, and business owners held once a quarter. The speaker was Dr. Eric J. Barron, president of Penn State University. Because he contributed to this book, I was looking forward to attending the breakfast and connecting with him in person.

His message to a room of 100 business leaders was fresh, unconventional, and very well-received. One man raised his hand when Dr. Barron was finished and said, "I have never heard a university president talk about the ideas and goals you've just shared. This is exciting!"

Dr. Barron came with a business message. He had written an op-ed in January outlining his vision for Penn State to be a driver of the economy. Not content to have PSU just incubate ideas, share knowledge, and foster critical thinking, he wants to see Penn State be able to move their $800 million in research funding to the marketplace.

"Penn State President Eric Barron wants you to know something: His University is a vast resource for the business community, and that resource is about to be unleashed," wrote Larry Portzline in the *Central Penn Business Journal* after the breakfast speech. The Invent Penn State program is a $30 million initiative, and Dr. Barron has set three goals focused on the intellectual property incubating on the Penn State campuses:

1. The University would be an economic driver.
2. The University would be instrumental in job creation.
3. The University was committed to student/career success— after the diploma.

"Colleges and universities have emphasized publishing for decades, but we can't hold knowledge too tightly. We need to get the products to the marketplace," he said. One of the first initiatives is to have Entrepreneurs in Residence and Mentors in Residence and to make access to capital a priority. Although funding research has not been the problem at Penn State, getting IP (intellectual property) to the marketplace will be a liberator for young students and a potential job creator.

Invent Penn State will "motivate faculty, students, and members of the community . . . to think about the economic relevance of their creative ideas and to envision themselves as successful entrepreneurs," states Portzline.

Keeping the high-paying jobs in the Commonwealth is also Barron's goal—and that's the goal of every university president and state Governor. Colleges in high gear provide every opportunity for students to reach their potential. Barron would like to see every student consider and have access to choosing Business as a minor because it strengthens a student's skill set and graduates a much more competitive student. Whatever career path you choose, understanding free enterprise, profit and loss, reading a balance sheet, tax codes—these are critical to success.

Discover the entrepreneurial ecosystem at your college. How can students graduate and get started in business? Are there entrepreneurs as adjunct professors? "We want to see ideas built from our $800 million in research," says Barron. Every university should be echoing the same sentiment.

FedEx CEO Fred Smith started FedEx as a college student. He famously said, "You absolutely, positively have to innovate—if only to survive." Smith wrote an economics paper on the need for reliable shipping in a tech world when he was a student at Yale University.

His professor, according to *Entrepreneur* magazine, responded: "The concept is interesting and well-formed, but in order to earn better than a 'C,' the idea must be feasible." From that improbable but high gear idea, Smith persisted and founded the world's first overnight delivery system and transformed the transportation industry. The first night of delivery, FedEx shipped 186 packages—not exactly a smashing success—but that didn't dampen his spirits and FedEx soon took off.

Today, FedEx, headquartered in Memphis where Fred Smith grew up, is ranked No. 12 on the list of Fortune's Most Admired Companies and is a $442 billion company—all from an idea created to solve a package delivery problem by a student in college.

Fred Smith is not alone in thinking high gear in college and finding a way to take his idea from think to build. You may recognize these powerhouse global companies that were started by college students, and some of them even dropped out of college to pursue their high gears.

Google, Facebook, Yahoo!, WordPress, Microsoft, Reddit, Dell, Dropbox, Kinko's, Snapchat, *Time Magazine*, and Napster are all businesses that were started by college students. Google, Facebook, and Yahoo! are three of the top four websites in the world—all founded by college students.

During their college years, my sons were constantly reminded by us to reach out to their professors, attend all your classes, do extra credit, send emails to professors if you need to discuss assignments or grades—it all matters I told them. The details add up to a big-picture view of a student, and that's what the professor sees. These are the relationships that open doors to high gear careers.

Offer to buy your professor a cup of coffee in exchange for a conversation about your career path; ask him or her to be a mentor; invite the professor to hear you perform or watch you compete.

For the cost of tuition, professors share knowledge, challenge assumptions, invest in research, and try to produce a well-rounded, inquisitive young learner who is prepared to add energy and ideas to the workplace. High gear professors are also able to help you connect the dots from campus to career.

Setting yourself apart from other students in the classroom is a high gear goal. Start tweeting some of the information you're learning. Start your own chats within your major (#PRchat, #STEMchat, #ChemChat, #EntrepreneurChat). If you're studying about the environment, business, music, entertainment, education, or chemistry, tweet your knowledge and you'll tap into the influence of high gear professors outside of the classroom, and they'll be able to retweet your content and help you build your online community.

Above all, don't be a passive learner. Come to the classroom ready to learn and expect a challenge. This prepares you to come to work with the same expectation. If you received a grade that you felt was wrong, make your case to the professor. Learning to present your value and engage in conflict resolution are skills that you'll need to reach high gear in your job. Because someone is a tenured professor doesn't mean he or she is flawless, nor does it mean he or she holds the only acceptable worldview or solutions to problems.

Tia Nichole McMillen is a very smart, high gear young lady who is a Public Affairs Specialist with the Navy Supply Systems Command in Pennsylvania. I met Tia years ago at church and later spoke to her class at Messiah College. She had asked me if she could visit my office to talk about how she should prepare for a career— she was only 19 or 20. She then asked me to meet for dinner after *Women in High Gear* was published to discuss her next high gear.

Tia soaked up every experience I shared, and I knew she would use it to reach her goals faster, and she would benefit from hearing about my own learning curves. A single mother, Tia has never let motherhood derail her or become a barrier to her career journey; in fact, I think her experiences as a mother have enhanced her educational journey. As she was rising in her Navy career, she really had a heart for education—college teaching to be specific. An opening came up for an adjunct professor at Elizabethtown College in Pennsylvania, and she applied along with about 100 other capable teachers. Tia received the job, and I reached out to her for some High Gear Professor advice. What would she tell her students about digging in and maximizing the college-to-career transition?

Tia Nichole McMillen's Fab Five

A new student is like a blank sheet of white, crisp, loose-leaf, paired perfectly with a bundle of newly sharpened pencils— the opportunities, with guidance and tenacity, are endless. As a lifelong learner and devoted mentee, there are five major areas I personally address with every degree, engagement, or endeavor.

I define these as the lessons most relevant to leadership and lifelong learning in general—those particularly relevant to where

I am in my leadership/learning journey and those that transcend any line of work.

1. **Understand office essentials.** Before you leave your career as a student to embrace your career as a working professional, know some key transition elements. These include making a mean pot of coffee; understanding business etiquette; knowing how to work a copier, shredder, printer; and improving your golf game. No, I'm not kidding. As the newbie on the team, nothing ethical is beneath you. When I was eight years old my dad signed me up for golf lessons and said, "You're going to be a strong female leader someday, and I don't want you to miss out on office decisions because you're a girl." What did this mean? It meant that some decisions are made during a round of golf, and I needed to be there. Whatever interests your boss should fascinate the heck out of you.

2. **Create a personal mission statement.** A little new age? Perhaps. However, I vehemently argue that without understanding who you are and the direction in which you wish to march forth feverishly, how do you get there? It can be simple yet all encompassing. My personal mission statement is: To authentically love God, love others, act upon these beliefs, and avidly answer Adventure's great temptations.

   Does this tell you where I work or how I serve? Nope. But it does tell you that I will make an impact and that I love a good challenge. It keeps me in line with my values yet encourages me to try new things. It's my blueprint for creating lasting impact. Develop your own mission statement that fits you and the great things you wish to accomplish.

3. **Put ethical decision-making at the forefront of everything you do.** Ethical decision-making begins with an understanding of self. It's developing a thoughtful personal mission statement, a personal vision statement, a personal brand statement, and a detailed plan of execution. It's conducting a thorough Strengths, Weaknesses, Opportunities, and Threats (SWOT)

analysis and acting upon discoveries. Still a little lost? That's okay. During your learning experiences, discern your moral compass. I have a mentor who explains moral excellence as "Good, Right, and Honorable."

Here is a checklist that I use to frame my moral compass.

- What does my decision say about my character? What perceptions can be garnered as a result of my action? Who I am and who I am perceived to be is important to me. One is only as great as his/her reputation.

- What are the pros and cons involved in my decision? This is when pure logic plays a role in my decision-making process. How are these pros and cons weighed by importance?

- Have I sought an outside, unbiased perspective? This is when I bring my decision to a trusted mentor. My mentor is an excellent example of someone who is ethical, just, and compassionate. He is the perfect sounding board for these questions. He knows my son and me well and is aware of both of our strengths and weaknesses. He provides sound advice with situational awareness and outside perspective—a hard blend to find in someone.

- Do I need to reconsider my decision? Part of my decision-making process occurs after I choose a path. I reassess that path to determine if I made the right decision. If not, I go through the process again and try to make a better one.

4. **Embrace emotional intelligence.** Emotional intelligence plays a key role in the success of any learner. Do you know your EQ? There are simple online tests you can take to figure out how your emotional intelligence is developing. Or, ask a professor! Over time, my students have taught me that their greatest emotional intelligence weakness is self-regulation. In order to best control your actions, strive to ALWAYS respond with intelligence and compassion instead of judgment. Here are

some examples of how my students have worked to improve their EQ:

- Apologize when wrong. My grandfather always told me, "A man (or woman) is not a failure until he blames his failure on others." We fail as leaders when we do not accept blame, sincerely apologize, and learn from mistakes. By taking due blame on yourself, you'll earn respect and be wiser in future actions.

- Remove what you hear and replace it with truth. So often we turn simple statements into pointed negativity. Assess what is actually being said instead of what you think you are hearing. Actively listen and clarify.

- Journal—with a twist. Writing down negative thoughts helps one visualize the petty issues that get in the way of success. Pull these negative thoughts from your mind and put them on paper. Then shred it.

5. **Find the right mentor.** Sometimes asking someone who you respect to mentor you is scary. My advice is to go straight to the top! Are you amazed by a particular CEO in the area? Maybe a particular professor? Perhaps you know a family member that you greatly respect but never really talked with. Here's a simple approach for establishing a mentoring relationship:

- ASK! Ask him or her to be your mentor. Find someone who is in a place in his or her life that you strive to emulate. Ask in-person if possible. If not, a handwritten note is always appreciated. Make sure that person understands why you are asking him or her to mentor you, and what you hope to gain from the relationship. Also acknowledge that your chosen individual is probably a very busy person, but you appreciate any time that they may have to spare.

- Follow-up. If your chosen mentor says Yes, schedule a meeting as soon as possible on his or her calendar. If they say No, thank him or her for their time and be courteous in correspondence.

- Send your new mentor your resume, perhaps some writing samples, goals, and your personal mission statement. Providing this information before your meeting will give your new mentor a chance to "get to know you" on paper and will prepare him or her for your meeting.

Mastering these five will help you make the transition from school to work. Don't be afraid to ask questions. Understand your story, your call to action, and what you bring to the table. Embrace lifelong learning. Build your own legacy. Use your talents for good. Encourage and empower others to do the same. Pay it forward, and don't look back!

CHAPTER 13

Advice from 35 Years of Experience as Business Owners

"Twenty years from now you will be more disappointed by the things that you didn't do than by the ones you did do. So throw off the bowlines. Sail away from the safe harbor. Catch the trade winds in your sails. Explore. Dream. Discover."

ATTRIBUTED TO MARK TWAIN

We hope you have enjoyed this book and find it helpful in seeking your high gear career path whatever stage you are in—student, graduate, job-seeker, mid-careerist, adult learner. We invite you to contact us and share your high gear stories. We'd love to hear from you and look forward to highlighting your journeys on our blog at www.StudentsInHighGear.com. Here are a few final tips and advice from our combined 35 years as business owners.

AMY

High gear is a life journey, and if we ever think we know it all, then we might as well hang up our capes. I have learned a lot from younger people, and I love to work with students. We have had a number of great experiences with interns, and some of them have turned into full-time positions post graduation.

Writing this second book is a high gear chapter for me in my career. As I write this, I'm torn between focusing on my client billable work, and finding the time to write this book. Not to mention I also have two teenagers and a husband. I must balance my time, and make sure I'm paying as much attention to my family and my client work as I am to this book. Yet, I know this book will be helpful to many, and it is an investment in me—my brand and my future.

Anne and I know that by promoting this book, we are advocating high gear in the workforce which ultimately helps our businesses. American businesses, small businesses, and even public service depends on the high gear thinking, actions, and the hard work of today's students.

Our tips and advice to students and graduates come from real-life work experiences. When you encounter challenges, the best advice I can give you is to get back on the path when you get bumped off it. Don't give up, and you must seek better in everything you are doing. If you run into a barrier, ask yourself if there are ways around it.

Setting the bar high pays off. For me, the bar was set when I quit my full-time corporate job and launched my own business in 1994. There is nothing scarier than knowing that you are responsible for generating revenue for yourself, your family, your employees, and their families. There is also nothing more liberating and satisfying than knowing that you can. It has not been easy, but success follows tackling challenges, making good choices daily, and connecting dots—continuous learning and acting. Move forward.

Make the most of your time. Time is the ultimate non-renewable resource—don't waste it.

Steve Jobs said, "Your time is limited, so don't waste it living someone else's life. Don't be trapped by dogma—which is living with the results of other people's thinking. Don't let the noise of others' opinions drown out your own inner voice. And most important, have the courage to follow your heart and intuition.

They somehow already know what you truly want to become. Everything else is secondary."

ANNE

If you've read this far, you have the DNA of a high gear employee or business owner. Whether you went to a technical school, Ivy League university, state university, community college, or are an adult learner in the School of Life, you realize you need to bring your A game every day.

I started my business at age 40 with no prior entrepreneurial or business owner experience. Zero. I refused to let that be a barrier to success or earning potential. Who asks for a loan at age 20 for a business idea? Someone with high gear intentions and the tenacity of a honey badger. It's the same DNA that drives a woman at age 40 to start a business and then to apply for an executive line of credit with no history of business ownership. It's your future to create, and we've included insights and experiences from every possible stakeholder in the student-to-career journey.

When I'm looking for student interns, I Google them and check out their online influence. I see who they tweet and what their images say about them. I expect my clients to do the same for me. In a Google Search, they will find my articles, social media content, TV interviews, pictures of concerts, and family events. They will find events I've created and organizations I lead.

Don't waste any time looking back and questioning why you chose a course or major. Begin today to map out your own strategic action plan. I never imagined I would be an entrepreneur, but I love this journey. At every opportunity, I spend time sharing my own challenges, failures, successes, and solutions with young men and women to help shorten their learning curves. Set stretch goals, and ask for help in reaching them.

"College education is an equalizer," says Dr. Linnie Carter, vice president, College Advancement at Harrisburg Area Community

College, the oldest community college in Pennsylvania. The same is true for the marketplace. I decided to start my own business because I saw two paths to prosperity as my sons were approaching high school: one was to work for an employer and be paid for my skills with an unlikely chance of exponentially increasing my earning potential; and the other was to work for myself and reap all the rewards of my hard work, including significantly increasing my earning potential. One was fairly stable; the other was fairly risky. One was a known; the other was an unknown.

When you set out on your own business journey, the marketplace will decide if your services are worth the fees. I chose to invest in myself and have reached a new high gear in 2015. I bought my own commercial building. That one decision and the corresponding commercial bank loan set in motion 32 economic transactions— people I have hired to help me renovate the property and go from purchase to occupancy.

It's gratifying to know that my decision to start my own business continues to have an immediate effect on fueling the economy, especially on a local level.

As you enter the workforce or pursue a new career, use the following tips as a launch pad:

1. Introduce yourself to smart business leaders and ask them lots of questions.
2. Join organizations like the chamber of commerce or alumni associations.
3. Volunteer in the community—help others.
4. Understand your value and confidently tell your story.
5. Choose a strong role model and mentor.
6. Protect your reputation and build a positive personal brand.
7. Be a Game Changer!

This book is peppered with the names of influencers and educators who have made a difference in our lives, not the least of which are our husbands and children.

We are grateful for our educational journeys and the people who selflessly opened doors for us and advanced our careers. In your high gear journey, you have at least two names—Amy D. Howell and Anne Deeter Gallaher—who will help you launch a new high gear and aspire to make a difference in your working world. Don't wait for your ship to come in, swim to it! High gear awaits!

Students in High Gear Workbook

YOUR GOAL-SETTING GUIDE

We believe that writing goals on paper helps establish a high gear mindset and will be a reminder of your short- and long-term goals. We hope you will refer to this guide often and update us along your journey.

What is your primary goal you hope to achieve after college graduation?

_____

_____

_____

_____

What are your career goals for landing your first real job?

_____

_____

_____

_____

What resources have you found at your school that can help you?

_____

_____

_____

_____

Have you formed mentoring relationships with your professors, and if so, who are they? What can they help you with outside of academics? Business introductions?

_____

_____

_____

_____

_____

Name 3 new ideas that you will explore to help you meet some business people in your college community, and how can you connect with them?

_____

_____

_____

_____

_____

What income are you going to need to attain after college to pay back your student loans? Year 1? Year 5? Year 10?

_____

_____

_____

_____

_____

Write down your Top 10 reasons any employer should hire you?

_____

_____

_____

_____

_____

_____

_____

_____

What questions will you ask when you interview for a job? How has the content in this book challenged you to think beyond the basics?

_____

_____

_____

_____

_____

_____

How are you thinking differently about communication skills and differentiating yourself from competing job seekers after reading this book?

_____

_____

_____

_____

_____

List the business publications in your community that you should be reading. Who are the editors and reporters at these publications? Can you find and connect with them on Twitter, Facebook, and LinkedIn?

_____

_____

_____

_____

_____

What do you think is the most important information to put in your LinkedIn bio?

_____

_____

_____

_____

_____

Find the leaders in your field on Twitter, Facebook, and LinkedIn
and follow them.

_____

_____

_____

_____

_____

What are specific strategies for using social media as you think
about a career or graduate school? Think about superconnections.

_____

_____

_____

_____

_____

Who are 3 business leaders who inspire you and why? Do you
follow them on social media? How can you connect with them?

_____

_____

_____

_____

_____

Find and subscribe to 3 popular blogs related to your interest of study and work. Start with Mark W. Schaefer's blog titled {grow} at www.businessesgrow.com and www.StudentsInHighGear.com.

_____

_____

_____

_____

_____

What do you think will be your greatest personal challenges in your career post-graduation, and how do you plan to overcome them?

_____

_____

_____

_____

Think of 2 people in business who would allow you to interview them for practice. Record notes from that interview and ask to stay in touch with them.

_____

_____

_____

_____

_____

What ideas do you keep wanting to pursue or know more about?

_____

_____

_____

_____

_____

What activities make you happiest and most satisfied, proud, and fulfilled?

_____

_____

_____

_____

_____

You have 140 characters to define your new aspirations and high gear goals. What will you tweet? Don't forget to add the hashtag #SiHG.

_____

_____

_____

_____

_____

Connect with us on Twitter at @HowellMarketing and @AnneDGallaher and follow the hashtag #SiHG for real-time insights and tips.

Acknowledgements

AMY D. HOWELL

To students everywhere, I hope you love this book and will refer to it often. You are our future! Go forward and do great things in high gear!

To my clients, who help me as much as I help them, thank you for trusting us to help tell your story. I have learned so much working with you all and am so happy that many of you are my high gear friends as well as clients.

To all of the great teachers and professors—past, present, and future—thank you for your passion and dedication. Your guidance, mentoring, and high gear teaching is needed now more than ever. We hope this book inspires you and recognizes you for the important job you are doing!

To my parents and sisters, thank you for your undying support always!

To Jim Howell, you are the strongest man I know! I love you more for surviving what most would not, and I am happy to be on this recovery journey with you! Your poise and dedication through an unimaginable nightmare and journey will be rewarded, and we are paving the way to help others . . . with *Healing in High Gear*.

To my two children, Bryan and Abby, you are gifts from God and my hope is that you achieve high gear as you navigate school and beyond. Stay that course and know we love you always and are so proud of you both.

To our many friends—in real life and across the globe—thank you for being there and being really great advocates for *Women in High Gear* and for us as business owners, mothers, and friends!

ANNE DEETER GALLAHER

Helping others and shortening the learning curves of those who seek to go where we've been is the purpose of our efforts here. How many times I've said, "If I only knew then what I know now, I would have been so much smarter!" It's our hope that everyone reading our book will gain a little more wisdom to make your journey safer, smoother, and more successful.

To my Father, thank you for teaching your children and grandchildren that learning never ends and that books, especially biographies, hold treasures of wisdom and experience to enrich our lives. And thank you, Mother, for loving us whether we earned a C or an A. You never saw a grade; you only saw potential.

To my husband, Corey, your example to our sons and to your students demonstrates daily your contagious love of learning. You'll never know how many young lives have chosen a career in chemistry because you ignited the wonder to explore and know more about our world.

To Joshua, Aaron, and Benjamin, you have taught me more about life than any college class I ever took or any parenting book I ever read. Your careers and willingness to pursue high gear goals defines the spirit of your generation. Dad and I remain your constant advocates.

To Mallary and Samantha, my daughters-in-law, you are extraordinary role models for this generation of learners. We are blessed to have you in our family. To Monica, thank you for your contagious optimism and spirit of adventure. You rock!

And to the most precious and youngest learners in our family, Easton and Hadley, I can't wait to see what you'll teach us!

A special shout out to my high gear clients and to Marisa Corser—your dedication to "powerful language" and your expert editing skills helped us refine our high gear message. I am grateful for your work ethic, friendship, and high gear role modeling.

Made in the USA
Lexington, KY
02 November 2015